THE NEW CHILDREN:
The First Six Years

THE NEW CHILDREN:
The First Six Years

Edited by John Travers

 GREYLOCK PUBLISHERS
Stamford, Conn.

CONTENTS

PREFACE

In November, 1975, Greylock Publishers organized a conference of nine scholars, all well known in their special fields and all dedicated to the welfare of children, to discuss their ideas about the development of the "new children."

The participants, in spite of their varied backgrounds, agreed that the early years of childhood should be their writing focus. Recent research, combined with carefully controlled observation, leaves few doubts about the impact of early experiences. If a child suffers deprivation during these years the physical, mental, emotional, and social effects may remain for life.

The task, as the authors of the following essays conceived it, was to gather the pertinent data emphasizing the significance of the early years, determine what techniques were most suitable to detect deficits in a child's background, and then discuss certain topics that are vital to a child's healthy development.

In the opening essay, John Travers summarizes the latest data about environmental influences on development. Using animal studies, malnutrition research, and human experiments, the author builds a strong case for the necessity of furnishing stimulating and enriching experiences for children. There are those, however, who question the environment's significance and who believe that heredity charts a child's course. Arthur Jensen is a good example of this view. But since we have some control over the environment, the author argues that we should concentrate upon helping parents create a stimulating and enriching environment for their children.

Gordon Ulrey, in the following essay, discusses the role of assessment to discover an existing or potential weakness in a child's performance. Recently, controversies have arisen concerning the nature of tests, especially intelligence tests. What do they measure? How valid are the results? Do they discriminate against certain youngsters? The author explores these and other questions in a wide-ranging analysis of psychological assessment.

In the third essay, Richard Schnell details ways in which skilled investigators can use psychological assessment to identify children's learning problems. He cautions us about the dangers of "labeling" children since a label may follow a child for life. The author then clearly categorizes and explains various learning handicaps, and also suggests preventive and remedial measures.

The socialization process has long interested Jessica Daniel and her concern is reflected in her essay of how socialization goes awry for some youngsters. Child abuse is a growing concern in our society, and the author attempts to identify the complicated causes of this phenomenon.

Ira Stamm's essay on play addresses the question "Why do children play?" Traditionally, answers have reflected the belief that children play because it is enjoyable, or they learn about themselves and their world by playing, or to adjust to powerful emotional experiences. Rejecting these either-or arguments, the author maintains that play serves multiple functions and presents both psychoanalytic and Piagetian theory to support his conclusion.

Morality has become an intense issue for Americans today. For whatever reason—Watergate, Vietnam, crime—people are searching for values that can guide their daily decisions. But parents also realize that a value system grows throughout a lifetime and consequently they desire guidelines for the moral development of their children. John Dacey, writing about moral education in early childhood, explores the work of Piaget, Kohlberg, Rath, and Simon.

The acquisition of an acceptable sex identity is one of the most critical accomplishments of childhood. In a society that currently questions "acceptable" sex identities and sex roles, boys and girls may feel frustrated in their quest for identity. In "Boy, Girl, or Person?" William Kilpatrick examines this changing concept by asserting that since sex differences exist we should weigh the biological and cultural evidence related to the causes of these differences. Then the author links his discussion to sex roles by questioning whether we should raise girls to be more masculine, boys to be more feminine, or simply raise children as persons.

Any discussion of children must confront the inevitable—television. Brian Brightly surveys children's viewing patterns, types of shows, and also includes an interesting discussion of the effect of commercials on children. The issue of television violence is carefully scrutinized with reference to the indecisive findings of the Surgeon General's report. The author focuses upon television as a teacher of the new children and offers suggestions for a more rewarding future role.

Finally, George Ladd discusses several developmental characteristics that parents and teachers can use in shaping an environment more suited to their children's needs. The author's chief contention is that children should be at the center of an educational environment that is conducive to growth. Since a child's environment is basically a scientific environment, the normal way for a youngster to discover his world is by scientific investigation, thus enabling him to expand his knowledge and bring order to his world.

The essays are all designed to inform students and parents (both present and future) about the importance of children's early experiences. If students are able to understand children better because of this text, if they are able to counsel parents more meaningfully as a result of our work, then all of us, authors and publisher, can take satisfaction in our efforts. It is through those students who will work with children and who will become parents themselves, and through today's parents that our growing knowledge and expertise will help the new children fulfill their promise.

John F. Travers

I.

EARLY EXPERIENCE AND INTELLIGENCE

By John Travers

What does it mean to say that early experience affects intelligence? Does it mean that we should surround children at birth with all kinds of gimmicks and gadgets, creating what the psychologist William James called "a buzzing, blooming confusion"? Does it mean that tender loving care comes before all? Something must explain such statements as "today's children are brighter than ever." Or, "look at today's knowledge explosion—a monument to man's progress."

No, that is not quite correct. We shall have to rephrase our statement: a monument to the progress of *some* men. Why must we restrict our statement to make it more precise? Is it because some men and women are naturally more gifted than others? Yes. Is it because some men and women receive greater opportunities than others? Yes. But it does not mean that *all* those whose opportunities are limited are less gifted than those who were the beneficiaries of more stimulating circumstances.

This brings us full circle to the ancient nature-nurture controversy.

Buried for so many years, it angrily burst forth in the late 1960s, with the work of Arthur Jensen and his belief that there are racial differences in intellectual performance. From the resultant heated controversy has come one agreeable consequence. Most (still not all) of the disputants agree that a child's early years are critical for healthy development into a mature, self-sufficient adult.

There are those who feel these years should provide the stimulation that enables a child to grow intellectually, to secure the foundation, both physiologically and psychologically, that ensures cognitive growth. There are those who disagree with this reference to intelligence and intellectual development, who feel that heredity tells all, but who are still willing to admit that the early years should provide a warm and accepting environment to help a youngster become an emotionally adjusted adult.

In the pages that follow, a strong argument will be made that a child's early experiences have a direct bearing on intellectual performance, achievement, and, ultimately, healthy adjustment. We do not intend to enter the debate over the intelligence test itself—does it measure an individual's intellectual capacity or does it measure achievement? Rather, when we refer to intellectual performance, or mental test performance, we are referring to scores on popular, frequently used tests such as the Stanford-Binet, or the Wechsler.

The logic of this essay should now be apparent: the early years are vital for maximum development. If the experiences of these years are deficient, then intellectual abilities, reflecting this deficiency, will suffer accordingly. We must qualify our statement by saying "accordingly" because there is no escape from our genetic endowment. Every human being differs genetically, which obviously results in varied human abilities.

There is no reassurance, however, that each child will fulfill his or her potential. Limited experiences mean limited development, both physical and mental. The American psychologist, Jerome Bruner, has said that one of the most important features of human development is the extent to which it is from the outside in as much as from the inside out.

Can we muster evidence to suport our optimistic conclusion that improving a child's environment will also improve intelligence? The encouraging answer is: yes. Both physiological and psychological studies show a clear pattern that we shall now trace. But danger signals fly concerning the time and duration of childhood deprivation and we must account for these in our discussion.

The Physiological Evidence

Recent advances in brain science provide knowledge that is especially significant for an understanding of the development of nervous tissue. Steven Rose, in his fascinating book, *The Conscious Brain,* states that one of the features that distinguishes the brain from other bodily organs is that the neurons will not regenerate, either in the child or the adult. We are born with nearly all of the neurons that we shall develop and the inescapable conclusion is that damage to any of these cells is irreversible damage.

The brain is the physical basis of our mental life and Nobel prize-winner, John Eccles, has stated that all mental activity, including the supreme activity of creative imagination, arises somehow from brain activity. Picture this brain activity: 10 billion neurons in the adult brain, capable of flashing signals instantaneously from one to another across synaptic junctions.

Eccles then asks the question that has intrigued man throughout his existence: what brain activity corresponds to the mind's activity and how does creativity burst into consciousness? Eccles speculates that repeated brain activation is necessary to establish vital neuronal patterns. Many and varied experiences are necessary for the child to build the physiological foundation upon which mental life depends.

Another Nobel prize-winner, Holger Hyden, has discovered that proteins play an important role in learning. Experiments demonstrated that nervous system proteins increased with learning, but after injection with chemicals that inhibited the formation of proteins, learning suffered significantly. Investigations also suggest that protein-deficient animals learn more slowly than those on a normal diet.

Do we have evidence that children suffer these same consequences when environmental conditions are deficient? If protein plays such a key role in learning, and if a child suffers from a lack of protein, it is reasonable to assume that learning and mental test performance will also suffer. Studies of malnutrition offer powerful evidence that this is precisely what happens. In the studies of malnutrition that we are about to analyze, two interesting comments constantly appear. First: malnutrition does not occur in a vacuum, which means that usually *all* elements of a malnourished child's environment are impoverished. Second: protein-calorie malnutrition produces results that are strikingly similar to the results produced by early environmental isolation. We shall return to both of these issues after examining the data.

One of the most severe environmental alterations, short of actual brain damage, is to deprive the organism of food. Joaquin Cravioto has conducted several longitudinal investigations of chronic malnutrition and his recent studies in Mexico have shown that adults deprived of food maintained their normal level of mental test performance until body weight declined about 30 percent. When malnutrition was eliminated, mental test scores returned to normal.

Unfortunately, the same is not necessarily true for children. All organisms experience critical or sensitive periods, during which proper environmental stimulation produces maximum growth. A lack of proper stimulation hinders growth, and in the case of malnutrition may produce damage. These critical periods seem to be times of rapid neurological growth and organization. Brain growth is an outstanding example of a critical period. From the last trimester of pregnancy to six months after birth is a time of great brain growth. It is also a time of great susceptibility to environmental experience.

The statistics of this period are particularly pertinent. At birth, the brain is about 30 percent of its adult weight. Estimates are that it weighs about 335 grams at birth, increases to 1064 grams at 2 years, 1190 grams at 4 years, and 1350 grams at 12 years. These figures and times are important since they indicate the time of greatest growth and potential vulnerability. As a result of his studies, Cravioto believes that if protein-calorie malnutrition occurs under 2 years and if it is sufficiently severe to affect physical growth, there is a real possibility of permanent mental and motor damage. Examining the physical increase in brain weight, we note that it coincides with the psychological findings of the American educator, Benjamin Bloom, who has analyzed longitudinal studies of intelligence and concludes that a child acquires 50 percent of his variance in adult intelligence by 4 years.

These and other speculations refer to the period of the brain's fastest growth. Steven Rose, the British physiologist, says that the sensitive period in human development that most affects subsequent brain development probably extends from birth to 18 months. But even for the next five years, prolonged malnutrition may retard subsequent brain development, but apparently less severely. The nutritionist, Sohan Manocha, states that it is only during the period of rapid brain growth that physiological damage ensues. If the brain achieves about 90 percent of its total growth by 4 years, subsequent malnutrition has little effect. The early peak of brain growth may be a blessing in disguise since most youngsters, especially those who are breast-fed, may achieve maximum brain development before malnutrition can leave its mark. Approximately 60 percent of the world's children between birth and 5 years are malnourished, but the percentage of mentally retarded children does not reach this same figure, which may well be due to the time of the brain's rapid growth.

What do these data imply for the purpose of this essay? Perhaps the most fundamental lesson that we can learn is that, although malnutrition definitely produces the effects we mentioned, it does not do so on a one-to-one basis. That is, malnutrition is associated with environmental conditions such as poverty, poor housing, disease, illiteracy, and a general lack of stimulation. The consequences of any, or all, of these circumstances are similar. For example, Manocha quotes a study conducted in India in which malnourished children's body weight was only 60 percent of normal. *But* their home environment was good (warm and affectionate); the children felt secure and had a sense of belonging. They played with pots and pans and other home objects. There was a good relationship between the parents. The IQ's of these children were as high as those from upper-class backgrounds.

A second implication relates to the time and duration of malnutrition and the extent to which recovery occurs after treatment. All evidence seems to suggest that if deprivation begins early and lasts for some time, the damage may be irreversible. If malnutrition strikes before 6 months after birth (actually within that 9-month interval we mentioned—the final trimester of pregnancy and the first 6 postnatal months) it may influence all subsequent development, both physical and mental. But when malnutrition occurs later, the results are better tolerated by the individual.

There seems to be a close similarity between the effects of malnutrition and social deprivation. Both frequently appear together; both produce similar results. It is difficult to separate the influence of one from another. Can we learn anything about the impact of early experience upon a child from the malnutrition studies? The answer is clearly, yes. If deprivation occurs early in life, and lasts long enough, a child may experience a lifetime of problems—physical, social, and intellectual.

Another conclusion that we can reach is that critical periods are indeed critical. Although it if difficult to specify precisely what critical periods are and when they occur, the evidence seems irrefutable that they exist. John Paul Scott, an investigator of critical periods, has conducted experiments with various animals that reinforce the critical period concept. He and his wife took a newborn female lamb into their home and reared her on a bottle. She became closely attached to the Scotts, "following them around like Mary's little lamb." After 10 days they returned her to the flock. She paid no attention to the sheep, would respond only to the Scotts, and three years later remained isolated while the rest of the flock gathered together. They had produced a social isolate.

Scott believes that it is an almost perfect example of a critical period: a brief duration when a small effort produces a major and lasting result. The Scotts then experimented with puppies. Investigators placed a pregnant bitch in a field surrounded by a board fence. After the puppies were born they were fed by attendants through a hole in the fence. The puppies had no human contact, perhaps a fleeting glimpse of a human through a broken board.

Individual puppies were removed at various ages and exposed to humans. Those removed during the first five weeks behaved normally and made friendly contact with people. Those removed at seven weeks manifested considerable shyness, while at 14 weeks the puppies had to be confined after removal because they were so wild. Based on this and many other experiments, the Scotts concluded that dogs have a critical period for social attachments—3 to 12 weeks. To emphasize the minimal effort required during a critical period, another study demonstrated that puppies will form normal attachments to humans with only two 20-minute contacts per week.

The thalidomide episode of the 1960s is a tragic reminder of human critical periods. Pregnant women who had used this seemingly safe sedative during the first six or seven weeks of pregnancy gave birth to youngsters who either had deformed limbs or missing limbs. This is a specific example of chemical interference with a critical period, in this case, formation of arms and legs. Women who had taken the drug later in their pregnancy produced normal children. The effect of German measles is equally as dangerous since it can result in blindness, deafness, or mental retardation during the first two or three months of pregnancy.

John Money's work with hermaphrodites at Johns Hopkins is another example of human critical periods. A girl, because of faulty hormonal action, is born with internal female sex organs (uterus, ovaries) but an apparent external male organ (penis). She is raised as a male before an accurate sex identity is made. After accurate identification and corrective surgery, she is now reared as a girl. Or consider the boy who has his sex reassigned (becomes female) because an accident caused removal of the penis. After surgery the child-rearing pattern is female. Will either, or both, of these children adjust to the change?

As Money says, we are now in the land of the Midnight Sun of sex. While these and other cases are fascinating, our concern is with the timing of the sex reassignment (usually a combination of hormonal and surgical treatment). Money believes that there is little chance of psychological adjustment after 3 or 4 years. He believes that the correct age for developing gender identity, although not quite from birth, begins with bright children at 6 months, and with almost all youngsters from 18 months. So the critical period is from the first months to 3 or 4 years.

> ...one has a degree of freedom to decide on a change during the first year to 18 months of life, but this freedom progressively shrinks with each month of subsequent age. The age of establishing conceptual language is also the age of establishing a self-concept. This self-concept is by its very nature, gender-differentiated (Money and Ehrhadt, 1974).

(William Kilpatrick discusses sex identity at greater length in a following essay.)

Herbert Birch, formerly of the Albert Einstein College of Medicine, has studied the relationships among malnutrition, environmental deprivation, and critical periods and concluded that to concentrate upon the child's biology is not to ignore the intimate relationship between a child's physical state and the environment. Surveying the malnutrition literature, Birch states that learning is not merely a cumulative process. Considerable evidence exists that indicates interference with the learning process at specific times (critical periods) causes immediate problems that could have future effects. Potential damage is not only a function of the length of deprivation. It is also a function of the time of deprivation.

A recurring theme in the malnutrition literature is the number of agents that are associated with a dietary deficit. One conclusion is that faulty learning may result from early malnutrition because the child is too apathetic to explore the environment, movement is restricted, and physical stimulation is lacking. Birch states that the malnourished child, or chronically ill child cannot respond to learning opportunities as the normal child does. So this lack of movement and its accompanying lack of stimulation may effect the central nervous system.

Richard Held's work at the Massachusetts Institute of Technology supports this interpretation. Held notes that anyone who has worn glasses initially experienced distortion, which may have been sufficiently severe to influence motor coordination. In a day or two, the condition disappeared—the nervous system adjusted so that vision through the glasses seemed normal and skillful motor coordination returned. As Held states, information from the environment must produce adaptation. Consequently, the central nervous system must adjust to the growth of the body (changes in distance between the eyes, between the ears), and our motor system must adjust to the bones' and muscles' growth to produce modified, more refined movements. For example, we know that it takes an infant only a few months to develop eye-hand coordination.

To test his hypothesis that the central nervous system adjusts to visual distortion, Held devised an experiment in which subjects wore goggles with prisms that made straight lines look curved. He then placed the subjects in a large drum that had an irregular pattern of small spots on the inner surface. The spots looked the same, with or without the prisms, that is, there were no straight lines on the drum which would appear curved through the prisms. Before entering the drum, the subjects all were able to identify straight lines. Upon entering the drum, the subjects (with goggles on) either walked around the drum for 30 minutes or were rolled around in a cart. Leaving the drum the subject removed the goggles and again examined the straight lines.

Held states that without exception the active subjects (the walkers) perceived curvature while the passive subjects perceived none. *The active subjects had adapted to the prisms; the passive had not.* These and other experiments mean that the feedback from movement influences perceptual coordination. It also means that youngsters too listless to engage in the ceaseless activity of the normal child will lack vital impressions in the central nervous system. If these impressions are not made at appropriate times, it is very possible that a critical period will be missed and all forms of learning may subsequently suffer.

There are obvious educational implications to our critical periods hypothesis. An American educator, Robert Havighurst, has formulated the developmental task concept, a series of tasks appropriate for certain developmental levels. He defines a developmental task as a task that arises at or about a certain period in the life of the individual, successful achievement of which leads to happiness and to success with later tasks, while failure leads to unhappiness in the individual, social disapproval, and difficulty with later tasks. We learn our way through life, and what we learn, and how successfully we learn depends on the timing and the quality of environmental stimulation.

Havighurst believes that the biological development of the body furnishes clues as to suitable biological-psychological tasks. If the individual does not achieve the task at the proper time, he may never achieve it successfully, or if he does, it will be with greater effort. Failure to achieve the tasks may cause partial or total failure in future tasks.

These tasks arise from physical maturation, cultural pressure, and personal choice. Havighurst hopes that the tasks he designated coincide with the age of special sensitivity for learning them. As he says, when the body is ripe, and society requires, and the self is ready for a certain task, the teachable moment has arrived.

There are developmental tasks for six periods: infancy and early childhood (0-6), middle childhood (6-12), adolescence (13-18), early adulthood (19-30), middle age (31-60), later maturity (60+). For example, the developmental tasks of infancy and early childhood are as follows:

(1)   Learning to walk.

(2)   Learning to take solid foods.

(3)   Learning to talk.

(4)   Learning to control elimination.

(5)   Learning sex differences.

(6)   Forming concepts and learning language.

(7)   Getting ready to read.

(8)   Learning to distinguish right and wrong and beginning to develop a conscience.

Havighurst's work reflects the critical period notion nicely. If muscles are not developed, toilet training remains erratic. If sex identity is not acquired during the early years, it remains a problem for life.

All of these influences—dietary, chemical, critical periods—stress the significance of the early years. But, can we reasonably say that psychological influences produce similar results?

The Psychological Evidence

The results of environmental deprivation, that is, a lack of a stimulating environment, are more difficult to determine. The authorities on malnutrition that we mentioned all agree that a barren social environment produces effects similar to those seen in the malnourished child. How can we test the accuracy of this assumption? Animal studies offer some pertinent data although great care is needed in applying their conclusions to the human.

Since the 1950s, investigators at the University of California,

Berkeley, have conducted studies that have startled the scientific and educational community while providing dramatic evidence concerning environmental stimulation and brain development. David Krech, Mark Rosenzwieg, Edward Bennett, and Marian Diamond are the people most closely associated with this project. Together, and individually, they have reported a consistency of findings for over 15 years.

Originally interested in the chemical changes that accompany memory and learning, the investigators were wrestling with an old question: does experience produce discernible brain changes? They reasoned that rats who had a stimulating environment with many opportunities for learning would eventually have a brain that differed from their impoverished brethren. (Krech humorously states that the investigators, assistants, graduate students, and thousands of rats, have labored—and some even sacrificed their lives—to find this evidence.)

The experimental technique was beautifully simple in its design: they randomly assigned some animals to an enriched environment, some to deprived conditions. Both groups had an identical diet but those experiencing the enriched condition lived 12 weeks in a cage and had many rat toys (levers to push, tunnels to explore, ladders to climb). The investigators instructed the graduate students to treat these rats with tender, loving care. Their poor, deprived mates were isolated individually in cages and placed in remote parts of the laboratory, devoid of attention. *But* the diet was the same.

As the investigators continued in their work, they were shocked to find that the brain weights of the two groups of rats had changed. Rosenzweig reports that the rats who had spent from 4 to 10 weeks in the enriched environment differed from the deprived rats in now possessing a heavier and thicker cerebral cortex, better blood supply to the brain, larger brain cells, and more glia cells. Enriched experience affected the ratio of cortical weight to the rest of the brain: the cortex consistently increased its weight in response to environmental stimulation.

Rozenzweig states that other investigators were initially skeptical of their results. But when repeated experiments for years produced identical results, some scientists swung to the other extreme: the brain is so plastic that any experience will modify it. This is not so. Rosenzweig notes that only the rats who actively interacted with the environment showed the increase in cortical weight, which leads to an important conclusion: an enriched, or stimulating environment, will produce the effects we mentioned only *if the organism interacts with the objects in the environment.* (This conclusion parallels Richard Held's work that we discussed: his subjects changed only if they actively interacted with the environment.)

As Rosenzweig says, there is now no doubt that many aspects of brain anatomy and brain chemistry are changed by experience. Krech agrees and states that a growing animal's psychological environment is of crucial importance for its brain development. If these results apply to the human, there are enormous possibilities for aiding youngsters from impoverished environments. And a secondary conclusion is almost as exciting. We have heard for a long time that "we learn by doing." Here we see the proof in Held's active subjects and those rats who actually interacted with their environment.

The evidence continues to mount that the environment and the timing of its stimulation is vital for development. Working at the Columbus Psychiatric Institute and Hospital of Ohio State, Seymour Levine poses a related and pertinent question: how do the stressful experiences of infancy affect the behavior and physiology of the adult? His basic assumption is that almost all the experiences of infancy involve handling by a parent or some other large figure, and this handling, no matter how tender, may involve stress. Levine traces his work to the 1950s when he subjected a group of infant rats to mild electric shocks. He placed another group in the shock cage but did not shock them, and he left a third group undisturbed.

Levine and his colleagues assumed that the third group would be the best adjusted of their groups. To their amazement, it was the third group—those not handled at all—that exhibited most problems. The investigators could not discern any differences between the shocked animals and those who were handled but not shocked. Both groups, as adults, seemed more emotionally mature, and learned new tasks more readily. Levine believes that stimulation, even painful, accelerates the maturation of the central nervous system. The brains of the stimulated animals possessed higher cholesterol levels and the animals themselves showed a more rapid rate of development.

Generalizing from these results, Levine states that while heredity undoubtedly determines the basic developmental patterns, organisms will not approximate potential except in interaction with a varied and stimulating environment. Levine believes that stimulation of the infant organism has "universal consequences" upon the adult's behavior and physiology. While we must be cautious in applying these results to humans, the author says that it is hard to conclude that these findings are limited to any particular species.

Some aspects of his work obviously trouble him. If painful stimulation produces effects that are indistinguishable from merely handling an animal, what does this imply for an adult picking up and petting a baby? Perhaps it means that infant stress is necessary for successful adult adjustment to the environment. Are there critical periods for stress? In Levine's studies there were: only those handled immediately after birth responded normally to later stimuli. Finally, he asks: is it possible to erase the effects of a lack of early stimulation (a critical period) by later, remedial stimulation? These are not easy questions; there are no easy answers.

It is time now to leave the animals and consider the available evidence about humans. Rene Spitz has conducted one of the classic studies of children from deprived environments. In 1945 he reported the results of an investigation of 164 children during the first year of life. The children came from four sources: professional homes; children from an isolated village where nutrition, hygiene, and housing were poor; a nursing home; and a foundling home. At the end of the first year, the children in the foundling home, although at about the same developmental level as the others at birth, had deteriorated.

Spitz states that these youngsters showed all the characteristics of 'hospitalism'' (both physical and mental). While hygiene and nutrition were excellent, from the third month the children showed extreme susceptibility to disease. An epidemic of measles struck the community and while the mortality was only ½ percent in the community, 13 percent of those up to 18 months, and 40 percent of those from 18 to 30 months of the foundling home children died. Only 2 of the children 18 months to 30 months could walk, talk, or eat alone. Some of these same children developed a weepy behavior that soon became withdrawal. They would lie on their cots with their faces turned away. They lost weight and suffered from insomnia. This behavior lasted for about three months, giving way to a dazed look, vacant eyes, frozen faces, unaware of what was occurring in the environment. Spitz calls this condition "anaclitic depression.''

Criticism of Spitz' work mounted as methodological weaknesses were exposed (selection of children, obscurity in details), but, interestingly enough, Spitz' findings have appeared so consistently throughout the years that today there is general acceptance of his conclusions. One of the conclusions is that while the youngsters' environment was unstimulating, it is mainly the lack of human partners, the lack of social stimulation, that produces the damaging consequences. This is especially true if a mother figure is missing. In Spitz' study, from 3 months on, the child must share a nurse with seven other children. He reasons that there is a time during which restriction of the mother-child relationship causes irreparable harm.

Another famous study is Wayne Dennis' report of children reared in an orphanage in Teheran. Infants were swaddled until 4 months of age; the sides of the cribs were covered so only ceilings were visible; there was one attendant for every 10 children, and toys were minimal. The average child usually sits alone at about 9 months—over 50 percent of the children in the orphanage did not sit alone until from 1 to 2 years. Most children walk by 2 years—of the orphanage children only 15 percent walked between 3 and 4 years. Where most children creep before they walk, the orphanage children rarely crept. When they begin to walk (between 3 and 5 years) the walking is preceded by a kind of scooting. While this study furnishes additional support to the belief that a lack of early stimulation causes physical and mental retardation, it does not supply evidence as to when damage will occur, what specifically causes the damage, or if the damage is irreversible.

But studies accumulate that point in the same direction: early experience affects physical and psychological development. Spitz reported his findings in 1945, Dennis in 1960. Lytt Gardner, writing in *Scientific American* in July 1972 reports on cases of what he calls "deprivation dwarfism.'' Gardner begins with the hypothesis that infants will suffer if their mothers are hostile to them or even indifferent. For example, in a British occupied German town after World War II, there were two municipal orphanages. Each had about 50 boys and girls from 4 to 14 years old. They had only official rations to eat and were below normal height and weight.

The matron in charge of Orphanage A was a cheerful young woman, genuinely fond of children; the Orphanage B matron was older, stern, who blatantly favored eight of the children. The Orphanage A matron left, and the woman in charge of Orphanage B was transferred to A, bringing her eight favorites. Until this time, the children in Orphanage A were superior to the others in physical development—taller, heavier. The switch in matrons coincided with the introduction of extra food for the youngsters in Orphanage A (unlimited amounts of bread, jam and concentrated orange juice.)

In spite of the extra food, the youngsters in Orphanage A showed *less* weight gain than those in B who had not received the extra food but who no longer had the strict matron. There was an exception. As you might expect, the matron's favorites exceeded all youngsters in physical development. Gardner concludes that the youngsters exposed to an unfavorable emotional climate reacted with a reduction in their growth rate.

He then gives a remarkable example of deprivation dwarfism involving twins. A mother gave birth to boy and girl twins. She then soon found herself pregnant again, undesirably so. Her husband lost his job and shortly thereafter left home. Until the time of the new pregnancy, the twins progressed normally, the boy somewhat more rapidly than the girl.

Soon a new dimension appeared: the mother's hostility toward the father was now directed toward the son. The youngsters were about 4 months old when the boy's growth rate slowed noticeably. When he was a little over a year, his height was that of a 7-month-old and his general condition required hospitalization. He immediately began to recover, and before the hospital released him, the mother and father had reconciled. The boy continued to recover and by 2 years his development matched his sister's.

Gardner speculates that environmental deprivation and emotional turmoil may upset the endocrine system, thus influencing a child's growth. He believes that there are sensitive periods in human development, similar to those in animals, although the timing and type of environmental stimulation needed for normal development are uncertain. Gardner concludes that deprivation dwarfism clearly demonstrates the ''delicacy, complexity, and crucial importance of infant-parent interaction.''

Thus far we have seen forceful arguments for certain conclusions: malnutrition affects physical and mental development, perhaps permanently if it is harsh and lengthy; lack of early environmental stimulation affects cortical development in animals; active interaction with the

environment affects the central nervous system; early emotional deprivation retards normal development. While we stressed the significance of
heredity in the beginning of our discussion, the studies presented make it
almost impossible to believe that heredity is everything—there can be no
normal development without environmental stimulation. But if stimulation is deficient, is the damage permanent and irreversible? Our lack of
hard data about the timing and extent of any deficit make simple answers
impossible. We must again accumulate evidence that suggest possible
conclusions.

One of the most fascinating of these studies was reported by Harold
Skeels in 1966. This study spanned a 30-year period. Two children, one
13 months with an IQ of 46, the other 16 months with an IQ of 35, were
removed from a state orphanage and placed in an institution for the mentally retarded. They were placed in wards with older, slightly brighter
girls and women, 18 to 50 years old, with mental ages ranging from 5 to 9
years. Six months after their transfer, Skeels revisited the institution and
was amazed to see these same two little girls running around, laughing
and looking like any normal children of their age. He immediately had
them retested and discovered that their IQ's had risen spectacularly.
They were constantly retested for the next three years and they maintained this increased mental level.

What had happened? Obviously, the environment caused the
change. Although placed with low IQ girls and women, the environment
was still more stimulating than the orphanage. They became the darlings
of the ward; the older girls and attendants lavished attention on them.
Thus the environment was more stimulating, affectionate, and conducive
to development.

Skeels next proposed transferring other orphanage youngsters to an
institution for the mentally retarded. Overcoming understandable op-
position, Skeels managed the transfer of 13 youngsters, all under 3
years. He was able to match a control group of similar youngsters who
remained in the orphanage. Every child in the transferred group showed
a substantial gain (7-58 IQ points) while all but one of the control group
showed a substantial loss (9-45 IQ points).

Skeels initially disclosed his findings in 1939, and, as with Spitz,
there were justifiable methodological criticisms. But the findings are sug-
gestive. In 1966, Skeels reported the results of a follow-up study of these
same 25 youngsters. This was about 20 years after the last examination of
the children. He managed to locate all 13 of the experimental group, and
11 of the 12 who had remained in the orphanage. One of this group had
died.

Skeels decided not to give them an intelligence test because of the
years that had intervened and the relationship to the first tests. Instead he
compared their adult educational and occupational level to the earlier
test scores. The two groups invariably followed the pattern indicated by
the initial test scores. The 13 members of the experimental group all were
socially competent—none was institutionalized. Of the 11 members of

the control group, 4 were institutionalized (one was mentally ill, three were in institutions for the retarded) and the others, with one exception, were in and out of institutions. The one exception was a successful typesetter for a newspaper in a community of 300,000.

What can we deduce from this study? *Early intervention makes a difference.* Skeels naturally draws these conclusions from his work but urges caution until we can identify the best means for intervening and the best techniques of intervention. He also makes the interesting comment that we should recognize that the child does not merely absorb the environmental impact but must intervene actively with it. Again we see the emphasis placed upon a child's active interaction with its environment.

Jerome Kagan, a Harvard psychologist, as a result of his studies of Guatemalan children, questions whether there is any relationship between cognitive development at 12 to 18 months and cognitive development at 11 years. Visiting remote Indian villages, he says he witnessed listless, apathetic infants; passive, timid 3-year-olds, but active, intellectually competent 11-year-olds. Consequently, Kagan states that the "capacity for perceptual analysis, imitation, language, inference, deduction, symbolism, and memory will eventually appear in sturdy form in any natural environment, for each is an inherent competence in the human person." This would seem to deny much of the importance of early environmental stimulation.

It is worth examining Kagan's study more closely to see if his conclusions apply universally. He worked in two Guatemalan locations. One was a subsistence village, moderately isolated, with Spanish-speaking residents. The other was an even more isolated Indian village, whose residents felt psychologically detached and alienated from the nation. Infants in the Indian village spent most of the first 10 to 12 months in a small, dark, windowless hut. Mothers did not work and remained at home. When they traveled to the market they left their infants with a relative. The child was constantly close to the mother, sitting on her lap, or carried on her back.

Kagan reported that people rarely spoke to or played with the children, and the only play toys were clothing, the mother's body, oranges, ears of corn, and pieces of wood and clay. These children manifested extreme motor passivity, fear, silence, minimal smiling and reminded Kagan of the tiny ghosts of the Spitz study. Children from the other location exhibited similar characteristics.

Kagan administered a series of tasks to both Guatemalan groups and the infants fared much more poorly than comparable American groups. But at 15 months, the Guatemalan children became mobile, left the hut, played with other children, and enjoyed a more stimulating environment. As the youngsters continued to age, their scores on cognitive tasks more closely approximated American comparison groups until the 11th year when children from both cultures were comparable. Kagan notes that the cognitive retardation observed during the first year of life vanished in the preadolescent years. He concluded that it seemed possible to reverse infant retardation caused by lack of stimulation.

If some economically impoverished American children do poorly on mental tests, Kagan's work offers hope that the damage may be reversible. As he says, if the first environment retards psychological development, the child will remain below normal as long as he remains within that environment. But if he encounters a more satisfactory environment, he is able to capitalize on these new opportunities and repair the initial damage. Kagan's results are encouraging. But questions remain. Is the environment of the village child actually deprived? He is never out of the mother's sight; she is in constant attendance to fulfill his needs; there is some physical stimulation. Perhaps Kagan's work serves to reinforce several other studies whose chief conclusion was that an emotionally secure environment was the essential element for normal development.

One cannot dismiss the duration of deprivation. Remember the children left the dark huts at 15 months. If, for the sake of argument, we agree that those past 15 months represented a deprived environment, the entry into the world at 15 months may have been well within the critical period for the development of those cognitive abilities Kagan later tested. For example, Kagan mentions Carmichael's famous study in which tadpole embryos were anesthetized until a control group began to swim. As soon as the swimming pattern appeared (about a week), he placed the anesthetized group in regular tap water and they swam as well as the control group. What Kagan does not mention is that when other investigators kept the embryos anesthetized for longer periods of time (about two weeks) the swimming pattern was permanently impaired. While Kagan's results are hopeful, we must interpret them cautiously: if deprivation is not too severe or too lengthy, then the child may possibly recover.

Implications of the Evidence

Both the animal and human studies that we have discussed indicate that early environmental stimulation is critical for healthy physical and psychological development. Presenting such studies places us squarely and perilously on the battle front, for there is heated controversy about the relative importance of heredity and environment. If heredity is all-important, then environmental circumstances, at any age, make little difference. Steven Rose asks that if one individual is genetically superior to another intellectually, does that mean we can do nothing environmentally to increase intellectual performance?

Beginning in 1969, and continuing today, the writing and research of Arthur Jensen seems to provide an affirmative answer to Rose's question. Maintaining that his studies show that intelligence is 80 percent inherited, the only logical conclusion is that if any race scores consistently lower than any other race on IQ tests, they must be genetically inferior intellectually. Such labeling of any group creates explosive tensions, especially if accepted as indisputable scientific fact, or if misinterpreted.

How does Jensen reach his conclusions? He assumes that intelligence exists, intelligence tests measure it, and IQ scores, derived from these tests, reflect intellectual capacity. There are practical aspects to this argument. Jensen states that after 5 or 6 years there is no better predictor of a child's future scholastic success than his IQ score. After 9 or 10 years, the IQ score shows a remarkably high correlation with both prestige and financial level of adult occupation. These findings are particularly important in a technological society and he believes that to reject IQ tests and scores is to reject civilization as we know it.

Based on studies conducted over the past 50 years, Jensen says that genetic elements are far more important than environmental influences in explaining individual differences in IQ. What are some of these studies? One, constantly used, involved the selective breeding of rats. By mating fast-maze-learning males with fast-maze-learning females, and slow with slow, the result eventually was two distinct strains of rats (with regard to maze-learning ability), one all fast, the other all slow. Twin studies are another favorite reference, especially identical twins reared apart. Although these twins were separated, their IQ's were more alike than fraternal twins reared together. Since identical twins share the same hereditary material, any differences in IQ scores must reflect environmental influence. Although the identical twins were in different environments, the closeness in IQ scores demonstrates the great thrust of heredity, minimizing the environment.

Jensen states that a reverse pattern also illustrates the greater importance of heredity. Adopted, unrelated children brought up in the same home differ from each other as much as unrelated children reared in different homes. That is, a similar environment has not brought the children to the same IQ level. These unrelated children from the same home differ from each other almost four times as much as identical twins brought up in different homes. The IQ's of the adopted children show little relationship to the IQs of their foster parents, but show almost the same relationship to their natural parents as any other child.

In his controversial article which appeared in the Winter, 1969 issue of the *Harvard Educational Review,* Jensen states that compensatory education has been tried and it apparently has failed. Efforts to raise IQ and improve scholastic performance have not succeeded. Blacks still score lower on IQ tests and we cannot attribute these differences to the environment, if, as Jensen says, intelligence is 80 percent genetically determined. There is no psychological and genetic difference between individual differences and group differences. We simply total the individual differences and they reappear as group differences. It is then that they become social and political dynamite. Consequently, we attempt to hide these real differences by attacking the IQ test, abolishing grading, and introducing a variety of administrative techniques: special classes for different children, eliminate the self-contained classroom, and re-examine our total educational system. Jensen believes that these "remedies" simply cover up a problem, rather than face it.

As you can imagine, Jensen's work has triggered dispute, demonstration, and demagoguery. There is no escaping his inevitable conclusion: intelligence is genetically determined; there are racial differences in IQ scores; therefore, there are genetically superior and inferior races. Consequently, if intelligence is mainly (80 percent) due to heredity, then we need not, indeed, should not concern ourselves with the question of early experience since it makes no difference.

There are, however, certain questions that challenge Jensen's hypothesis. In the following essay, Gordon Ulrey will discuss the uses and abuses of psychological testing, and the various interpretations of intelligence testing. Here we shall raise a fundamental question about the IQ test: does it assess capacity, or is it actually an achievement test? When you examine the items in any mental test, the dependence upon cultural attainment seems obvious.

Jensen's work rests largely upon studies in which the Stanford-Binet Intelligence Test was used. This is understandable since the Stanford-Binet is one of the most widely used IQ tests *but* blacks were never included in its standardization. Is it possible, or even fair, to compare blacks with whites on this test? Many other questionable techniques are involved when the two racial groups are compared. For example, black youngsters will score higher when the tester is also black. Rose argues that while IQ scores for American blacks are undoubtedly lower than whites, it is scientifically impossible to conclude that this is a genetic distinction. Such a conclusion is possible if we limit our discussion to the genetics of a single population, containing a common gene pool. Even then we could speculate about difference solely within *that* population. It tells us nothing about another population. Rose also finds it a naive argument that assumes an identical environment for blacks and whites. A black is black in a white culture. The same applies to a lower-class child in a basically middle-class culture. Common sense dictates that we include these differences in our analysis of differences in IQ scores.

The American psychologist, J. McVicker Hunt has said that while we cannot absolutely rule out the possibility of racial differences, the issue remains unimportant while some youngsters, black and white, live in poverty with limited opportunities to learn. Hunt rejects the argument that there are real differences between intelligence and achievement tests. While there are differences, they are differences in degree. Intelligence tests are not as limited to academic curricula as are achievement tests, but school experience contributes heavily to the IQ score. Both reflect a current performance level that clearly reflects previous learning. A youngster who is culturally deprived is a youngster who has restricted opportunities to learn, thus influencing IQ scores.

Benjamin Bloom has examined several of the classic longitudinal growth studies and attempted to determine how much of the variance in adult intelligence appears during the early years. (The longitudinal growth studies are those that have re-examined the same individuals during many years, some for as many as 30 years.) He found an interesting pattern of relationships: intelligence measured at age 1 has no correlation with intelligence at age 17, at age 2 the correlation is .14, at age 4 it is .71. By age 11 the correlation with intelligence measured at age 17 is .92. From these data came the famous, although slightly inaccurate statement, that 50 percent of adult intelligence is present by age 4. As Bloom notes, this amazing statistic suggests the rapid growth of intelligence during the early years and *the possible great influence of the early environment on this development*.

Bloom then states his belief that intelligence is a developmental characteristic, and that IQ scores reflect an individual's general learning, which also reflects an individual's opportunities to learn. These opportunities either enhance or restrict verbal learning, interactions with the environment, encouragement of independent thinking, and motivation for intellectual endeavors. Environmental influence seems to be greatest during the early periods of intellectual development, and least in the later periods. Bloom estimates that the effects of extreme environments (both deprived and enriched) on intelligence is about 20 IQ points—which could be the difference between a productive life or a life in an institution! George Ladd in a following essay offers some suggestions about the environment as a treasure of scientific information for the child—for any child.

Herbert Ginsburg refers to the "myth of the deprived child" and states that many psychologists mistakenly believe that a poor child's intellect is deficient. Relying heavily upon the Swiss psychologist, Jean Piaget, Ginsburg concludes that there are cognitive universals (patterns of language and thought) shared by all children. While there are social class differences in cognitive development, they are superficial differences. Regardless of cultural and social differences, children pass through the sensorimotor, pre-operational, concrete operational, and formal operational stages of cognitive development. Piaget's work, and the cross-cultural studies that support it, is encouraging for, if there are these cognitive universals, as Ginsburg states, then there exists the possibility of improving a child's intellectual performance, especially if intervention occurs early enough.

Conclusions

After presenting only some of the classic and most recent research and opinion, what can we conclude from our discussion? The basic question is not how much does the environment influence development, but *does* it influence development? It would be ludicrous to dismiss the overwhelming mass of evidence that we have mustered. If the environment influences, then what difference does it make if mental test scores are 99 percent genetically determined? Since we are not ready to begin human genetic manipulation, all we can do is change environmental conditions. Scientifically, let us by all means continue our efforts to distinguish the effects of the two. Socially, politically, and economically, let us face reality. We can change the environment; let us begin.

We must intensify the efforts to specify what environmental experiences, at what age, produce specified effects. These efforts should inform future research and speculations since disagreements have arisen which increase our perplexity. Why do the data of some studies almost force us to stress the mother-child interaction? Why do other studies emphasize social interaction, so that the mother's role is secondary? Why do some investigators state that the physical aspects of the environment are all-important? Why do still others urge active interaction with the environment?

We must also examine a deprived environment more carefully. Recall Ginsburg's skeptical expression, "the myth of the deprived child." Bruner has recently stated that it is doubtful if a deficit exists in minority group children, and any differences that appear are superficial differences between different cultural groups. That is, if there is a good diet, warm relationships, and active interaction with the environment, the environment is far from barren. It may be *different,* but not *deficient.*

But experience—both physical and psychological—affects development. In the final report of the Harvard Pre-School Project, recently released, Burton White says that he would like to make the bold statement that the mother's direct and indirect actions with her 1- to 3-year-old child, especially *during the second year,* are probably the most important influences in the development of a pre-school age child. When White initiated this project, he never intended to study infant development. Rather, using Bloom's magic age of 4, his research group concentrated upon youngsters 3 to 6 years. But after repeated testing, they reached an amazing conclusion: they were too late!

The competencies they were testing were present by 4 years. They then turned their attention to the childrens' homes and attempted to identify those experiences that make a difference in a child's development. They found the difference: the mother. The effective mothers talk constantly to their children, consciously or unconsciously structure the environment to encourage interaction, and physically handle the child, thus fostering security. Jessica Daniel, in her essay on socialization, presents some fascinating, if depressing, data explaining what happens when the socialization process falters.

The study of barren environments is of worldwide interest. In a massive survey, Britain's *National Child Development Study* measured the growth and development of children born in England, Scotland, and Wales during the week of March 3 to March 9, 1958. 15,000 children were studied at regular intervals for 15 years. Data came from schools, medical clinics, family and social service agencies, plus testing and interviewing the children.

The British investigators defined a disadvantaged child as one suffering from the handicaps of a large, low-income family with over-crowded living conditions and one parent missing. These criteria applied to one of every 16 children. Any one of these conditions could be catastrophic for a child; the combination usually produces predictable negative results. The mother's poor physical condition caused health problems for the child: their general physical development was inferior; school achievement lower. These youngsters were predominantly white but exhibited the same problems as some American blacks and non-English speaking children. The conclusion is inescapable: deprived children come from strikingly similar backgrounds.

The report concludes by speculating not whether Britain can afford to help its deprived, but whether it can afford not to help them since poor developmental conditions are disastrous for child, family, and society. If, as the report suggests, environment is mainly responsible for these developmental difficulties, it makes all attempts at early intervention worthwhile. Incidentally, or not so incidentally, the title of the report is *Born to Fail*.

Early experience counts.

REFERENCES

There are several pertinent, readable books that you may well enjoy examining in more detail.

Bruner, Jerome S. *The Relevance of Education*. New York: W. W. Norton and Co., Inc. One of America's (now of Oxford, England) leading psychologists, this collection of essays reflects Bruner's variety of interests and offers some telling comments on early deprivation.

Havighurst, Robert. *Developmental Tasks and Education*. New York: David McKay, 1972. This is a popular paperback that describes Havighurst's interpretation of critical periods and what they imply for education.

Manocha, Sohan. *Malnutrition and Retarded Human Development*. Springfield, Illinois: Charles Thomas, 1972. An excellent overview of the nature, extent, and effects of malnutrition.

Money, John and Ehrhardt, Anke A. *Man and Woman, Boy and Girl*. New York: New American Library, 1974.

Rose, Steven. *The Conscious Brain*. New York: Alfred Knopf, 1973. A challenging look at man's brain and the consequences of the information. Readable and exciting.

II.

PSYCHOLOGICAL TESTING OF YOUNG CHILDREN

By Gordon Ulrey

When the "Gesell norms" were first published in the 1940s many parents naturally compared their own children to these norms. If Dr. Gesell said, "most children are able to walk by 12 months", many concerned parents of non walking 1-year-olds concluded that their child was "subnormal" or "retarded". The Gesell norms were reported as 50th percentiles (or median). This is a score indicating that 50 percent have reached a certain level and 50 percent have not. Therefore, the chances that children will walk at or before 12 months are just 50 percent. Insufficiently described information or poorly understood facts about children may be dangerously misleading. Developmental milestones such as walking, head control, or first words occur within a wide range of normality and also vary according to racial and cultural differences. It is well known that a little knowledge may do more harm than good and this is especially true of information about a young child's behavior and development.

The pioneering work of Gesell has contributed significantly to our understanding of children's behavior and those agents that facilitate or thwart normal development. For the past 10 years Dr. Berry Brazelton and his collegues at Children's Hospital in Boston have been developing a psychological test for newborns that is administered as early as the first day of life. The test measures differences in the child's adjustment to his new environment by observing his recovery from unpleasant stimuli, such as a pin prick, loud bell, or rattle. It also measures a child's orientations to his surroundings such as turning to the sound of a human voice. The test has revealed variations among newborns that indicate individual interactions with the environment. For example, variations in an infant's cuddling response make some babies more pleasant to hold than others. This may have far reaching influences on the formation of the parent-child relationship and other social relationships. While this scale yields interesting information, it has still not been clearly established how measured behaviors are related, if at all, to future developmental factors such as intelligence. As our knowledge of child development has improved, a variety of psychological tests have evolved that make meaningful behavioral assessment of children possible at very early ages.

There are observable changes in interests and in the kinds of stimuli which motivate children to follow directions and solve problems. These make it necessary to use different tests for different age levels. The tests and test procedures that are appropriate for infants in the first year of life are not appropriate for the preschool child from 3 to 5. An examiner who is competent to test one age level, such as elementary age children, may not have adequate skills for testing the lower age levels. The implications of a 3-year-old withholding speech are different from a 6-year-old doing the same. Most behaviors are appropriate at one age level, while others may be pathological when they occur at a different age level. The potential for misinterpretation or misuse of test data is a serious problem in testing younger children, and precautions must be taken to insure appropriate use.

There are special problems and numerous difficulties in early testing, but when used appropriately, these tests have proved to be invaluable tools for early identification of developmental difficulties. In medicine, the early diagnosis of a disease increases the probability of obtaining a cure. From this medical model we assume that early identification and treatment of developmental difficulties increases the potential for successful remediation. Tests for younger children now make massive screening possible. And diagnostic testing can increase the likelihood that all children, even those seriously handicapped will achieve more of their potential. This chapter will describe the tests and procedures that are appropriate for children ranging in age from early infancy to 6 years of age, as well as some of the related problems and issues. The term "psychological testing" is used here in broader sense than intelligence testing, because a wide spectrum of behaviors are measured that do not always correlate well with intelligence.

Psychological Testing

A psychological test is a systematic measurement of behavior that makes possible the comparision of individual performances. The results may be useful for describing a child's developmental status or estimating ability. Testing involves the study of a very small sample of behavior within a limited period of time using "standardized" procedures. Test items and problems are presented to all "subjects" using the same procedures. This makes it possible to make meaningful comparisons of the behaviors. Interpreting test results is like observing a very small section of an object and determining what the whole shape will look like. The procedures for measuring behavior are more complex than taking an individual's pulse or temperature. Numerous environmental and internal variables influence results. An examiner must elicit an optimum performance from a child in order to obtain a reliable estimate of his ability or an accurate description of his developmental status. This is more difficult with younger children. To use a psychological test effectively the examiner must have an appreciation for as well as an understanding of standardized procedures and informed judgment of the extraneous variables that influence a given performance.

A wide variety of instruments are used for systematic measurement of behavior. These include interview questionnaires, observation checklists, group-administered personality and cognitive tests, projective tests, developmental screening tests, and individually administered intelligence tests. All of these are tools for obtaining data about the developmental level of an individual. Most of them, however, are designed for school age children and are not useful with pre-school age or infants. Several textbooks provide comprehensive reviews of the various tests. (See Anastasi, Cronbach, and Robb, *et al.)*

Psychological tests are either administered individually or the same test may be given to a group. Usually, group tests are used for screening large numbers of school children for intelligence or achievement levels. For the school age child, individual tests should be given *only* when some type of learning or behavioral problem has been observed, rather than for screening purposes. Unfortunately, there are no reliable group tests for children under the age of 6 because of the difficulties in eliciting an optimum performance, and wide variation in verbal skills. Therefore, all screening and diagnostic testing of children under 6 years of age must be individually administered.

Individual testing is needed for pre-school age children and infants to insure the selection of appropriate testing difficulty, to facilitate appropriate responses, and to assure attention to the tasks. To elicit a child's best performance the examiner must present items at a pace that is appropriate to the child's attention span and speed of response. The testing situation must be tailored to each individual to obtain a reliable and optimum performance. With the individual test much more can be learned about the child than his successes and failures. Individual test performances reveal such things as how well a child follows directions, his reaction to success or failure, the kinds of activities he appears most comfortable with, the consequences that reinforce him, his ability to organize and solve problems, and many other specific weaknesses or strengths related to learning skills.

But individual tests can only yield this data when the examiner is well trained. The potential yield from individual tests increases as the examiner's ability to discriminate between abnormal and normal responses to given tasks improves. The examiner must know the procedures for administering the test, the underlying theory of the test, and its potential uses and limitations. Because of the various age differences in attitudes and intellectual functioning, different procedures and training experiences are needed to yield useful information from diagnostic tests of children under 6 years of age. Although screening tests for young children must be individually administered the examiner does not have to be as highly trained for identifying behaviors that suggest developmental difficulties at the mass screening level. The background, theory, potential uses and limitations of individual diagnostic and screening tests will be discussed below.

The use of psychological testing evolved from an interest in measuring differences among people as well as differences in the same person at various times. An early investigator, Francis Galton, created a controversy with his "psychology" laboratory at the International Exposition of 1884 in London. He paid people to participate in activities which measured keenness of vision and hearing, muscular strength, and reaction time. Galton believed that tests of sensory discrimination and reaction time were a measure of intelligence. Most of the early experimental work attempted to measure mental ability or intelligence. While he did not develop an acceptable test of intelligence, Galton made great advances in quantifying behavioral data.

The first psychological tests were used to identify mental retardation. The first important intelligence test was developed in 1905 by Binet and Simon to measure the differences between Parisian school children with subnormal mental ability and children who had adequate intelligence but were "too lazy" to do their school work. This scale, after several major revisions, was translated and revised again by Lewis Terman at Stanford University where it became known as the Stanford-Binet Intelligence Scale. The concepts of mental age and the intelligence quotient have given the Binet test wide-spread appeal and also have made it the subject of a great deal of controversy. The earliest attempts to develop pre-school and infant tests of intelligence were based on revisions and adaptations of the Binet test. Problems with instability of test scores, the unpredictability of later intellectual performance (e.g., school achievement), and disagreement as to the meaning of results, such as IQ scores, have led to more recent improvements and revisions of the Binet. These difficulties with testing concepts and uses will be discussed later in this chapter.

Developmental Screening

Studies of child growth and development that utilize behavioral tests can describe many of the expected patterns for children at different age levels. These studies have also increased an understanding of factors that precede and affect the development of clinical syndromes. There are many variables, both biological and environmental, that may predispose an individual to developmental disabilities. Some knowledge of a child's developmental history and a brief behavioral assessment can be used to screen a child who is "at risk" for abnormal development. The concept of "at risk" is used to describe a child who has a high probability of becoming developmentally handicapped. While the technology for determining which children are at risk is available, most problems are not discovered until a child manifests learning difficulties in school. Programs are needed that will detect the at risk child earlier than school age. Such programs should plan experiences to improve, remediate and maximize the child's development. Several pilot screening programs have already been devised for mass screening and treatment of children as early as infancy. From these programs we have discovered strengths and weaknesses of mass screening.

An overview of the issues related to comprehensive screening on a wide scale was presented by John Meir in 1972. It is assumed in massive screening programs that the responsibility for recognizing the child who is developing abnormally must include a variety of professionals in the public health services (family doctors, nurses, etc.) Systematic effort is needed to locate and screen children at the community level who may not be involved in a regular health care facility. An example of an outreaching screening program is the La Junta Parent-Child Center program that serves the Arkansas Valley area. This program involves an Advocacy Component that sends trained "parent-educators" on home visits to screen children who are not receiving regular health care. This service subsequently serves as a catalyst and coordinator of resources needed for further evaluation and intervention. The children progress through the various levels of care depending on their special needs.

A general model for systematic screening of preschoolers would involve four stages of testing, each increasingly more comprehensive. At *Stage I* brief tests and interviews would be completed by paraprofessionals for gross sorting of children at risk developmentally. *Stage II* would involve a professional psychologist examining the at risk children to sort out the "false positives," or those erroneously screened as abnormal. This stage would also refer a child for more specialized and comprehensive testing when indicated. *Stage III* would involve a team of specialists evaluating the child and recommending the appropriate treatment. *Stage IV* would specify treatment and a follow-up program to monitor the child's development. Periodic retests of the norms and the efficiency of the screening are needed to decrease the probability of "false negatives" or those erroneously screened as normal. The success or failure of each stage depends on the instruments used and the training of the people using them. What is being measureed as well as the special problems in psychological testing of young children must be understood by everyone involved at each level of the program.

The existing tests for children under 6 years of age vary considerably in their scope and purpose. These range from gross screening (Stage I screening) instruments that can be administered by a paraprofessional to the comprehensive diagnostic tests which require special training to administer (Stage III). Stage III testing involves several tests and a team of specialists in other disciplines to determine a definitive diagnostic evaluation and prescribe an educational program. The available psychological tests vary in terms of standardization, age level appropriateness, intended uses and limitations, types of items, and the underlying models of human development.

Test Concepts

Numerous concepts such as mental age and IQ have evolved from psychological testing that are central to an understanding of how each test can be used appropriately. Several of these concepts will be discussed below.

Mental Age

The Stanford-Binet Intelligence Scale (Terman and Merrill, 1960) is one of the most widely used psychological tests today. It was developed from the work of Simon and Binet in 1905 and has evolved to its present form through numerous translations and revisions. This scale was developed to determine which children in the Paris School System lacked the necessary intellectual skills to achieve in regular classrooms. The determination was made by comparing the performances of children on numerous "school related tasks" at different age levels. The 1908 version of the scale extended from 3 years of age to age 13 and introduced the concept of *mental age* (MA). This concept facilitated interpretation of the test results and helped make the test very popular. Mental age is determined by what the average child of a given age level is able to successfully complete on the test. Binet and his workers presented various tasks arranged in order of increasing difficulty to a group of French children. From the early testing they were able to determine how many tasks the average five-year-old could complete. Other children who completed the same number of tasks were assigned a mental age of 5 years. Therefore, mental age was defined as the number of tasks successfully completed by an average child. Children then could be assigned to grade levels according to their mental age level.

The mental age concept can be misleading, such as when a 3-year-old scores an MA of 3 and a 6-year-old also scores at the 3-year level. While the scores are the same, the thinking processes and types of items passed may differ. The 6-year-old child's physical and social experiences will have been different than a 3-year-old's, making their interests and motivation quite different. When substantial developmental lag in a child's mental age is measured (Stage II testing) more information about the child's deficits and learning strengths is needed to determine his educational needs. An understanding of why a child obtained a given mental age is more useful than just comparing his scores to others. Information obtained from individual testing, such as attention span, degree of interest in doing well, and the child's approach to problems in general should be studied. Perceptual-motor and social maturity measurements are needed as well as testing by other specialists, such as audiologists and speech pathologists when indicated. A team of evaluators is required at Stage III to do a complete diagnostic evaluation and plan the appropriate intervention.

Determining if a developmental delay is significant or within normal limits can pose a problem. This is resolved by statistically examining the relative standing of a child to the performance of a representative sample of children at the same age level. The distribution of a large sample of test scores from a given group will appear on a graph as a bell-shaped curve or the well known "normal curve." (See Figure 1.) Most people score near the middle where the average or mean score is, while fewer scores occur in the lower and higher ranges. A child's performance can be compared to the norm according to how much it deviates above or below the mean score. His relative position or rank compared to others is also described. The variance of scores of a normal curve can be described in standard deviations which correspond to fixed percentages of scores that typically fall within a given range from the mean. For example, most scores, or a little over two thirds (68 percent) occur within one standard deviation of the mean, while only about 2 percent fall between two and three standard deviations from the mean. The significance of a very high or low score can be thought of in terms of the percentage of scores that are likely to occur that far from the mean. Generally, when a child's developmental progress is delayed two standard deviations or more, the lag is considered significant.

Intelligence Quotient

To obtain an index score for comparing performances, each child's MA can be divided by his chronological age (CA) and multiplied by 100. For example, the average 5-year-old child would score 100.

$$\frac{MA = 5}{CA = 5} \times 100 = 100$$

This ratio score is referred to as the intelligence quotient (IQ). When the CA equals the MA a child is progressing at the "average" rate. Early studies indicated that the ratio IQ's may be misleading because of differences in the variance from the mean at each age level. For example, a delay in MA of 1 year for a 2-year-old will be very different than a 1-year delay for a 6-year-old. Therefore, a more meaningful and accurate measure of a child's relative performance would express his score by

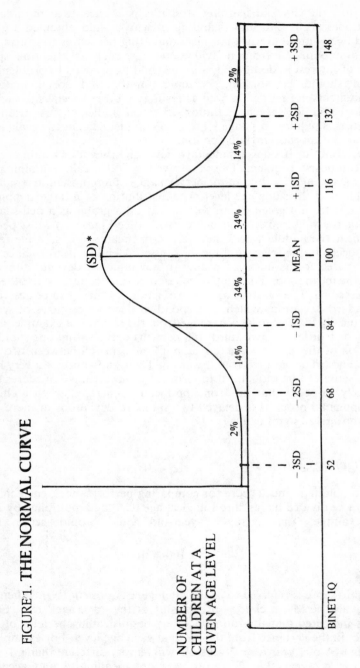

FIGURE 1. THE NORMAL CURVE

*Standard Deviation

standard deviations from the mean for each CA level. This is referred to as the deviation IQ and is employed with most major intelligence tests in use today. To facilitate the statistical comparisons of scores, the standard deviation for all the Binet IQ's are fixed at 16. This in effect means that 100 ± 16 (84 to 16) represented 68 percent of all childıen within the average range of mental maturity or intellectual functioning. Most of the standardized tests provide tables for the conversion of MA into a deviation IQ.

The IQ index has become almost synonymous with the word *intelligence* because of its wide scale use. What does the IQ actually measure and what does it mean? The answers go back to the origins of the test and the original test items chosen. Binet believed that intelligence was the ability to make good judgments. He did not base his test on any model or theory of intellectual development. He simply chose tasks that required judgments similar to those used in school work. Various tasks were tried and through trial and error and some statistical analysis, a cluster of tasks at various age levels was discovered that successfully predicted school performance for most children. Therefore, a child's performance (IQ) became an indication of the probability of his doing well in school. This was assumed to reflect his general intelligence.

The Binet scale was translated and revised by Terman in 1916 and standardized on a large sample of Americans. The test has been used widely to detect children with intellectual deficits and has been one of the most successful for predicting school performance. In its present form it is used for ages ranging from 2 years through adulthood. The norms represent a broad cross section of American culture, and the test consists of six items at 6-month intervals until the 5-year level when there are six items for each 12-month interval. These items are mostly verbal with some performance items (blocks, beads) at the younger levels. It is one of the most popular tests for children between 2 and 6 years among clinical psychologists.

There are several limitations and potential problems in using IQ scores. The biggest danger is when IQ scores are used inappropriately to exclude various individuals from educational experiences and opportunities. Some object to the continued use of intelligence testing on the grounds that the tests are culturally biased and thus discriminate against some ethnic and racial groups. For example, the Binet has a disproportionate number of verbal items that can substantially misrepresent the performance of a child for whom English is a second language. Total reliance on that child's Binet performance could be very misleading. The problem is more often with how the test is used rather than the test itself. Misuse may result both from unreliable administration of items and the insidious use of the IQ score for inappropriate labeling and school placements. To avoid this problem *no child* should ever be given a Stanford-Binet test unless a specific problem is indicated and the test is administered by a trained examiner. Another important limitation of the Binet IQ score is that prediction of academic success decreases for children under 6 years of age. The apparent instability of intellectual performance by preschoolers makes accurate assessment of intellectual ability difficult.

Developmental Quotient

In the 1920s when many researchers were working on the development of the Binet test and the concept of a general intelligence, others were beginning to develop tests for even younger chidren. There were numerous attempts to design downward extensions of the Binet for testing infants (0-2 years). However, the major pioneer of infant assessment was a physician, Arnold Gesell, whose early work with testing infants contributed significantly to the developmental evaluation of very young children. Between 1925 and 1949, Gesell and his colleagues compiled large amounts of data and designed techniques for systematically measuring the course of "normal" development from early infancy through 5 years of age. In 1927, they began a long range study of the growth and development of 107 "normal" infants. The subjects were described as middle-class, native born, and of northern European extraction. They were examined at intervals of 4, 6, and 8 weeks, and then after every 4 weeks until they were 56 weeks old. Testing was done thereafter at 1½, 2, 3, 4, 5, and 6 years of age. The famous *Gesell Developmental Schedules* were developed on the basis of the data from these 107 children. Obviously, this sample does not represent a wide cross section of American children. The norms are very limited and are not appropriate for children of different backgrounds. Variations in the sample of a limited population may bias an average and should always be taken into consideration when interpreting the results. Growth charts of different social and ethnic groups show systematic differences in rates and averages.

The Gesell Schedules include a variety of simple tasks and observations of behaviors in four general areas of development: Motor (Gross and Fine), Adaptive, Language, and Personal Social. The occurence of behavioral patterns and milestones (e.g., smiling, rolling over, cooing) at the expected times are assumed to reflect normal development and the unfolding maturation (genetic) of the child. The underlying model for development places more emphasis on biological (nature) growth than the differential effects of environmntal experiences (nurture), but does not deny the importance of the environment. Gesell was primarily interested in the rate of maturity in each area as an indicator of normal psycho-neurological development. He assumed that skills in all four areas were important for normal mental development.

Gesell's technique puts a strong emphasis on the appearance of behavioral patterns as they correspond with chronological age. He introduced the concept of a developmental quotient (DQ) to express the overall rate of development of a child. The DQ is the ratio between maturity age (behavior occurring at certain age levels) and the actual age, therefore:

$$DQ = \frac{\text{maturity age}}{\text{chronological age}}$$

The DQ serves as an index of the child's current rate of development and can be used to diagnose handicaps in young children. Gesell refers to "maturity age" rather than mental age because his emphasis is on the overall developmental picture of a child.

Besides the poor standardization sample there are several other limitations to the Gesell test. The test was designed primarily for developmental evaluations done by physicians. Interpretations require at least a minimal knowledge of neurological and physical development factors in children. Also, the scoring of items requires subjective clinical judgments since the procedures for administering and scoring are not objective enough, making agreement among examiners difficult. Many of the personal-social items are influenced greatly by family experience and training. This scale would be appropriate only for an experienced examiner of younger children in Stage II or Stage III developmental evaluations. Most clinical psychologists use the more recently developed infant tests.

Reliability and Validity of Test Scores

Responsible use and interpretation of a psychological test such as the Binet must take into consideration both the reliability of the assessment and the validity of what the test purports to measure. The competent examiner must be aware of the basic psychometric properties of the test being used. Briefly, reliability refers to the consistency of measurement, while validity is how well a test measures what it was designed for. The reliability of a test can be lowered by both errors in the testing procedures and extraneous variables affecting the child's behavior such as anxiety or motivation. Comparisons of test performances over short periods of time (one or two weeks) indicate a certain degree of instability in scores with variations of as much as 20 or 30 IQ points reported. Test manuals usually report a range of error which appears to be inherent in the test measurement to allow for expected variations in scores. For example, the Binet test is reported to have an inconsistency of about plus or minus five IQ points, which means a score of 100 will range from 95 to 105 because of error in measurement alone. It is most meaningful to report IQ scores as ranges since two scores within 10 points may differ by chance only. It is more difficult to obtain a reliable test performance from a preschooler or infant because of a greater inconsistency in their behavior and motivation.

The validity of a test can never be any better than its reliability. Validity is an important issue in psychological testing because a test score may not represent what the test was designed to measure. To test for validity one must examine the relationship between test performance and other independently observed behaviors. For example, two separate tests of intelligence should yield similar results on the same child. One problem with testing young children is finding tasks that validly represent intellectual skills or deficits. In general, intelligence tests for children under 6 years of age do not consistently predict future cognitive achievement. Because of the limited validity of these tests, their usefulness is limited to the diagnostic and clinical judgment of child psychologists.

Types of Tests

Infant Intelligence Testing

The Cattell Infant Intelligence Scale is a downward extension of the Binet Scale. It also includes some items from the Gesell Schedules. The test was developed to measure the intelligence of infants and children too young for the Binet. The Cattell scale extends from 2 to 30 months. The test arrangement consists of items grouped according to age levels, with 1-month intervals during the first year, 2-month intervals during the second year, and 3-month intervals during the first half of the third year. It is scored similarly to the Binet with a mental age and ratio IQ A child scoring at or above the 30-month level is then administered Binet items to complete his testing.

The standardization of the Cattell was done over a long period of time on 274 children who were retested at the ages of 3, 6, 9, 12, 18, 24, and 36 months. The subjects were from lower-middle-class families, as determined by income and occupation of the fathers, and were of northern European descent. This sample was broader than Gesell's but is still biased socially and ethnically. The administration and scoring of the Cattell scale is more objective than the Gesell scale. Similar to the Binet, the test yields mental age which can be converted into a ratio IQ. There are no deviation IQ tables available for the Cattell.

The most appropriately standardized and objective test for measuring infant intelligence in use today is the Bayley Scales of Infant Development. Nancy Bayley and her workers spent about 30 years (1940s-1969) developing this test. The test consists of three subscales designed to evaluate mental skills, motor skills, and social-emotional maturity. The mental and motor scales are scored separately and both consist of items arranged in ascending order. The items are from earlier tests (Gesell, Cattell) with a few new ones added. It was standardized on a sample of 1262 children in various subgroups—sex, race, socio-economic status, rural-urban residences, and geographic region—based on the 1960 census. The socio-emotional scale was not included in all the sampling and is more subjective than the other two scales. It is interesting to note that although the samples were quite different, a study by M. T. Erikson, *et al.,* in 1970 indicates that the Cattell and Bayley are virtually interchangeable for the clinical assessment of infants.

The Bayley is scored by an accumulation of items passed (raw score) which can be converted into a score similar to an IQ referred to as a PDI (Psychomotor Development Index). Bayley refers to the PDI as an index of "psychomotor" skills to emphasize the combined cognitive skills and motor skills rather than "intellectual" skills. During infancy it appears that cognitive skills have not been developed enough to measure them without also measuring motor skills. Therefore, psychomotor seems more appropriate to emphasize the interrelationship of motor and mental skills.

But a unified score such as infant IQ, MA, or PDI, does not describe the deficits or strengths that contribute to the score. For example, an infant may score a significant delay because of any one or combination of the following deficits: affective, visual, fine motor, cognitive, auditory deficit, or a home environment with little stimulation. While the tests do not differentiate or identify the deficits, a skilled clinician can learn much about the child's strengths and weaknesses through observations of the testing performance. The standard administration of an infant test to a developmentally handicapped child involves special difficulties and should only be done by a trained examiner who can vary the testing procedures to learn more about the child.

The concept of a general score to indicate an infant's (0-2 years) intellectual level has been seriously challenged because of the poor prediction of later intelligence. Infant tests measure mostly preverbal or psychomotor skills which appear to have only a limited relation to later adult intelligence. A recent volume, *Origins of Intelligence,* (1976) provides a comprehensive review of the concept of infant intelligence.

The validity of infant tests has been scrutinized by examining the relationship between a score at one age level and a similar measurement taken several years later. This relationship is called predictive validity. The research on the predictive validity of infant tests indicates that infant IQ stability in normal populations is poor, with correlations between infant tests and school age tests ranging from -.16 to .49. However, infant test scores in subnormal (clinical) populations are more stable than other test scores. While predictive validity has been significant with groups of children scoring in this low range it is not adequate for individual prediction. When other factors along with test scores, such as socio-ecnomic status, sex, and parent-child relationship differences are used in conjunction with test scores the predictive validity improves. The main limitation on the validity of infant tests is the lack of items that are "pure" measures of cognitive ability. This makes children with other handicaps difficult to test and frequently makes them appear to be functioning at a lower level than they are capable of.

Pre-school Intelligence Testing

The Wechsler Preschool and Primary Scale of Intelligence (WPPSI) was developed for use with children between the ages of 4 and 6½. It is a downward extension of the very popular and successful Wechsler Intelligence Scale for Children (WISC) which is used for children 6-16 years of age. The WISC includes five verbal and five performance subscales which yielded much more useful information than a single IQ score. Wechsler and his colleagues found that below the age of 4 cognitive abilities could not be comparatively analyzed as subskills that would correlate significantly with adult intelligence. They concluded that it is not possible to assess children's intellectual potential below the 4-year level with the same approach used with older children. Many test items correlated well with a given age but were not associated with later cognitive ability.

While the WPPSI is not useful with the very young child, it has been used extensively to evaluate late preschool and kindergarten level children. The format of verbal and performance subskills allows the examiner to develop a comprehensive picture of the child's intellectual strengths and weaknesses. The validity of the WPPSI scores is still not impressively demonstrated although the verbal IQ correlates well (.76) with the 1960 Binet scores. The WPPSI was standardized on a good representative sample of 1200 children. Both the WPPSI and the Binet tests are appropriate for Stage II or Stage III diagnostic testing of preschool age children.

Test of Sensorimotor Development

A general ability concept appears to be insufficient to describe the abilities of young children. Traditionally, an index of intellectual ability is determined by an accumulation of all the items passed with no account given for why answers are missed or any explanation of the underlying processes that influenced the failure. The famous Swiss psychologist, Jean Piaget, began working on this problem in the 1920s and has made significant contributions toward a better understanding of it. He views the cognitive development of children as an unfolding of progressively more complex thinking skills which are formed by the interactions between biological growth and environmental experiences of the child. The level of the child's thinking skills are inferred from his apparent awareness of his surroundings (sensory) and subsequent actions (motor) which are described as sensorimotor behavior. The child's perception and thinking about his environment are assumed to progress through predictable levels of sensorimotor activities which can be elicited by testing procedures. For example, a child will learn that objects exist even when they are not visible in the following order: (1) visually following an object, (2) noticing the disappearance of a slowly moving object,

(3) finding the object when partially covered, and (4) finding the object when completely covered. Based on Piaget's theory of cognitive development and predictable sequences of sensorimotor behavior, Ina Uzgiris and J. Hunt have developed a new test of infant intelligence.

The Uzgiris and Hunt Scale consists of six subscales with items arranged in ascending order of difficulty and are assumed to be ordinal. Ordinal means that on a given subscale, a child must be able to perform all the preceding tasks before the next level of difficulty can be achieved. The six subscales measure the sequences of different sensorimotor skills. The subscales with brief examples are as follows: (1) visual pursuit and object permanence (see example in above paragraph); (2) understanding of means-end relationships (repetitions of actions producing spectacle, letting go of an object to get another, use of locomotion as means); (3) development of imitation: visual or gestures (imitation of familiar action, imitation of unfamiliar action, imitation of gesture invisible to the infant); (4) understanding of operational causality (repetition of action producing a spectacle, use of a specific action to produce a spectacle, behavior repeated in a familiar game); (5) construction of object relations in space (recognizing the reverse side of objects, relationship of container and contained, stacking blocks); and, (6) schemas for relating to objects (drops, throws, wears, hugs).

The development of the test and the procedures for administering the items are described in *Assessment in Infancy*. This test is unique in that no norms (items correlated with chronological age) are used to interpret the results and no quantitative score is obtained. Norms are not used because all children are expected to progress through the same sequence of tasks "sooner or later" and only their level of progress is reported. The examiner is then able to write a description of the child's level of functioning on each subscale. This provides a profile of the child's strengths and weaknesses without comparing him to other children. It should be noted, however, that the consistency of the sequences of behaviors on the subscales has not been clearly demonstrated experimentally, although some supportive data has been reported. The test is appropriate for infants between 2 months and 2 years of age.

One advantage of this test is that no score such as an IQ or DQ is reported and the problems inherent in relating an infant's performance to a general intelligence concept is avoided. The test simply facilitates the study of those factors that may support or retard progress in intellectual development. After an examiner determines an infant's level of skills on a given subscale he can then plan appropriate stimulation to foster the development of sensorimotor skills. Examiners working with parents of handicapped infants can focus on what the child is able to do, rather than comparing his performance with other chidren's. Parents are told what kinds of activities their child will be able to do next and what kinds of stimulation will facilitate his development. This approach has potential and is beginning to be used for planning infant education programs and for monitoring the successes and failures of the experience. It would be useful to extend this type of planning and stimulation to the preschool age level.

One limitation of this scale is that diagnostically it is appropriate only for Stage III testing and requires a comprehensive understanding of cognitive development for interpretation of the results. It does not indicate degrees of developmental handicaps which means that other tests such as the Bayley or Cattell must also be administered. There are very few tasks that an infant under 6 to 8 months can perform, which limits the usefulness of the test. Further research is needed to determine the relation of the subscales with future intellectual development and school performance.

Psychological Test for Neonates

The Brazelton Scale, discussed earlier, is an innovative test designed for assessing differences in behaviors during the first four weeks of life. Test items are designed to elicit patterns of coping with environmental stimuli. The patterns are rated on a continuum scale rather than a success or failure record. This yields useful data which makes possible systematic comparisons of the behavior of different newborns. The varying behaviors reflect the varying degrees to which children interact and cope with their environment, a different perspective from the traditional view of determining how the environment affects the child. For example, newborns vary considerably in their ability to "shut out" aversive stimuli such as loud noise. A child who can quiet down (habituate) and disregard a repetitious noise will be reacted to differently by parents than the child who continues to cry and be upset for much longer periods of time. Besides the affect on the parent-child relationships, the ability to habituate may also indicate differences in cognitive processing. A child who habituates to the noise faster may be processing the information more efficiently and therefore be more "intelligent." But much more research is needed to demonstrate the relationships between the Brazelton test items and future psychological development.

One problem encountered when testing infants is their state of awareness. Their level of alertness and activity will vary all the way from being asleep to being wide awake. A child's awareness can vary according to how close it is to nap time or feeding time. To account for these different levels of activity, the Brazelton Scale is administered first with a child asleep, state 1, and proceeds with various items through state 4 which is the most active and alert state. Certain items are only appropriate when a child is in a specific state, such as state 1 (deep sleep) when the number of responses to a stimulus are observed and other potential distractions are minimized by the state of sleep. These procedures have made it possible to attain a high level of agreement among examiners ($r = .90$).

This approach to psychological testing of infants is still very new and needs further development, but it appears to have numerous possibilities. It can improve our understanding of how children influence the parent-child relationship and can suggest ways for parents to cope with difficult infants. There also may be some factors that predict future intellectual abilities, including those factors that may be identified as potentially handicapping. This scale is important because it is the earliest possible psychological test for identifying children who are at risk developmentally. There is a need for the development of scales for older infants using these same general procedures.

One limitation is that examiners require special training and must be able to screen the infant for normal reflexes before giving the Brazelton test. The examination is time-consuming and is begun only when the child is sleeping. It is most appropriate for Stage I or II development evaluations. Before this scale proves more useful diagnostically, the relationship between the test performances and later psychological development must be examined more closely.

Perceptual-Motor and Social Maturity Scales

Other tests for young children that are usually included under the category of psychological tests are perceptual-motor and social-emotional scales. These tests are most useful when given in conjunction with individual intelligence tests for the Stage III level of developmental evaluation. These tests are scored on the basis of age level norms which makes comparisons with intellectual functioning very informative. For example, a child with average intellectual ability may do poorly on an intelligence test because of a perceptual-motor deficit that affected his performance of several tasks. The examiner could detect this by noting the specific items failed or recognizing a discrepancy between the child's level of intellectual skills and his perceptual motor functioning. The most commonly used test for perceptual motor skills with children under 6 years of age is Beery's scale of Visual Motor Integration.

The most widely used test of social-emotional maturity is Doll's Vineland Social Maturity Scale. It is primarily a test of self-help skills but it also reveals a child's level of emotional maturity and personal adjustment when administered by a trained examiner. The test norms extend from early infancy through adulthood. Information for the test is gathered by interviewing the parent and observing the child. It is most useful for comparing a child's intellectual level and his social maturity level to detect adjustment difficulties. For example, a child who appears to be distractable and has a short attention span, may have a parent who has been very permissive or has placed unrealistic expectations on the child. This behavior is likely to lower his intelligence test performance making it an unreliable estimate of his ability. Information from the Vineland Scale can be used by preschool teachers as a standard schedule of normal development, measuring individual differences to screen for developmental difficulties, and a measurement of improvement following a new educational experience. This information could also be passed on to the parents to help the home meet a child's special needs.

Non-verbal Intelligence Tests

Intelligence tests for preschool and school age children are best used to predict school performance. A young child's verbal skills are the best single indicator of his eventual academic achievement. One of the primary reasons that infant tests do not reliably predict later intelligence is due to the fact that few if any verbal communication skills are developed in infancy. Children with delayed language development or a language handicap present a special problem because an estimate of their intellectual ability is difficult. To cope with this problem, several non-verbal intelligence scales have been developed. One example is the Draw-a-Person (DAP) test which is scored according to the amount of detail a young child puts in his drawing. Other tests include the Merrill Palmer Scale of Mental Tests (18 months-6 years) which provide performance items, puzzles, and form responses for children who may have language difficulties. The norms for this scale must be used with caution because they are based on a small sample and have not been revised since 1931. A more recent scale is the Columbia Mental Maturity Scale (3½-9½ years) which measures general reasoning ability, and requires no verbal responses. None of the non-verbal scales have a high level of predictive validity for later intelligence and should be used only for Stage II or Stage III evaluations with other measures when possible.

The Screening Tests

There has been a proliferation of developmental screening instruments during the past 10 years. The primary purpose of screening tests is to identify the "at risk" children among all segments of our population as early as possible, especially those who do not routinely come to clinics or hospitals. The effectiveness of any screening program is dependent on the test being used and how it is administered. In general they are all administered individually and may be done by a paraprofessionals with a minimal amount of training.

Screening tests themselves vary in time required and their comprehensiveness. Four of the widely used screening tests are discussed below in order of increasing comprehensiveness. The *Rapid Development Screening Checklist* (Giannini, *et al.,* 1972) is a list of two or three major developmental milestones at various age levels, ranging from 1 month to 5 years. For example, at 9 months, "can the child say 'Ma-Ma' or 'Da-Da,' " or at 5 years, "can he follow three commands?" The *Guide to Normal Milestones of Development* (Haynes, 1967) is a chart that indicates several important milestones at selected age levels ranging from the 1-month to 36-month levels. For example, at the 6-month level the child should be able to "...sit with minimal support" or "roll from supine to prone," etc. The *CCD Developmental Progress Chart* (Boyd, 1966) focuses on different levels of functioning in the areas of motor skills, interpersonal-communication skills, and self-sufficiency skills ranging from birth to the 8-year levels. Several behaviors are observed in each area and include items such as, at the 3-year level "...balances on foot for five seconds, separates without fuss, and buttons self." The *Denver Developmental Screening Test* (Frankenburg and Dobbs, 1966) examines behaviors in developmental areas including gross motor, fine motor-adaptive, language, and personal social ranging from 1 month to 6 years. This test indicates the percentages of children expected to pass items at a given age level allowing for normal variation in developmental milestones. For example, children are expected to "imitate speech sounds" between the 6th and 11th month with 50 percent doing it by the 8-month level. (See Figure 2.)

Screening tests utilize the concept of developmental milestones to detect children who are not developing certain behaviors by an expected age. Behaviors are measured either by questioning the parents, observing the child and eliciting behavior, or some combination of the above. There is some disagreement on the norms, based on the type of sample they were tested on. The best approach is to use a test that was standardized on a sample as similar to the subject as possible. The tests also vary in how the range for behavior occurrences is expressed. Some are based on the latest point at which the bahavior can appear in the average child, while others, such as the Denver, report a range or percentile.

Screening tests should never replace a diagnostic evaluation. The screening is never any better than the follow-up diagnostic and intervention recommendations. The above screening tests are appropriate for Stage I testing only.

Use of Tests

Children are generally aware that they are being tested and will respond accordingly. For the younger child, and especially infants, the examiner must construct situations that will elicit the desired responses. A major variable in the testing procedures is the rapport established between the examiner and the child. A concerned parent may say, "Oh, you will never get her to do that now because she just ate. She does it beautifully in the evening, just before bedtime when we play with her." An anxious 4-year-old may expect to get a shot or experience some other discomfort if he is brought to a hospital or a doctor's office and may refuse to cooperate in hopes of avoiding the discomfort. It is important for the examiner to develop a relationship which will help a child overcome his resistance to testing. The examiner must be familiar with a wide range of behaviors in order to deviate from standard procedures when children are difficult to test or when a child's handicap makes these procedures inappropriate.

Examiners need to be sensitive to how their own behavior affects

FIGURE 2.

1. Try to get child to smile by smiling, talking or waving to him. Do not touch him.
2. When child is playing with toy, pull it away from him. Pass if he resists.
3. Child does not have to be able to tie shoes or button in the back.
4. Move yarn slowly in an arc from one side to the other, about 6" above child's face.
    Pass if eyes follow 90° to midline. (Past midline; 180°)
5. Pass if child grasps rattle when it is touched to the backs or tips of fingers.
6. Pass if child continues to look where yarn disappeared or tries to see where it went. Yarn
    should be dropped quickly from sight from tester's hand without arm movement.
7. Pass if child picks up raisin with any part of thumb and a finger.
8. Pass if child picks up raisin with the ends of thumb and index finger using an over hand
    approach.

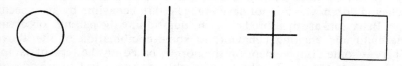

9. Pass any en-closed form. Fail continuous round motions.	10. Which line is longer? (Not bigger.) Turn paper upside down and repeat. (3/3 or 5/6)	11. Pass any crossing lines.	12. Have child copy first. If failed, demonstrate

When giving items 9, 11 and 12, do not name the forms. Do not demonstrate 9 and 11.

13. When scoring, each pair (2 arms, 2 legs, etc.) counts as one part.
14. Point to picture and have child name it. (No credit is given for sounds only.)

15. Tell child to: Give block to Mommie; put block on table; put block on floor. Pass 2 of 3.
     (Do not help child by pointing, moving head or eyes.)
16. Ask child: What do you do when you are cold? ..hungry? ..tired? Pass 2 of 3.
17. Tell child to: Put block on table; under table; in front of chair, behind chair.
     Pass 3 of 4. (Do not help child by pointing, moving head or eyes.)
18. Ask child: If fire is hot, ice is ?; Mother is a woman, Dad is a ?; a horse is big, a
     mouse is ?. Pass 2 of 3.
19. Ask child: What is a ball? ..lake? ..desk? ..house? ..banana? ..curtain? ..ceiling?
     ..hedge? ..pavement? Pass if defined in terms of use, shape, what it is made of or general
     category (such as banana is fruit, not just yellow). Pass 6 of 9.
20. Ask child: What is a spoon made of? ..a shoe made of? ..a door made of? (No other objects
     may be substituted.) Pass 3 of 3.
21. When placed on stomach, child lifts chest off table with support of forearms and/or hands.
22. When child is on back, grasp his hands and pull him to sitting. Pass if head does not hang back.
23. Child may use wall or rail only, not person. May not crawl.
24. Child must throw ball overhand 3 feet to within arm's reach of tester.
25. Child must perform standing broad jump over width of test sheet. (8-1/2 inches)
26. Tell child to walk forward, ⟨⟩⟨⟩⟨⟩⟨⟩→ heel within 1 inch of toe.
     Tester may demonstrate. Child must walk 4 consecutive steps, 2 out of 3 trials.
27. Bounce ball to child who should stand 3 feet away from tester. Child must catch ball with
     hands, not arms, 2 out of 3 trials.
28. Tell child to walk backward, ←⟨⟩⟨⟩⟨⟩⟨⟩ toe within 1 inch of heel.
     Tester may demonstrate. Child must walk 4 consecutive steps, 2 out of 3 trials.

__DATE AND BEHAVIORAL OBSERVATIONS__ (how child feels at time of test, relation to tester, attention
span, verbal behavior, self-confidence, etc,):

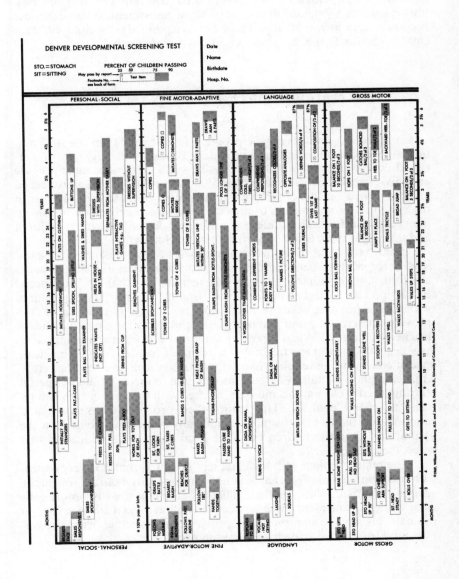

DENVER DEVELOPMENTAL SCREENING TEST

children and the testing situation. Clinical training for administering tests to children with special learning difficulties must include the development of an awareness of how the examiner's behavior influences the child's performance. The experienced clinician can use his own testing style as a "standardized" variable in assessment. As an examiner becomes more aware of how his or her behavior affects children, each child's reaction to that behavior is a useful measurement.

Treatment and Follow-Up Services

A screening and diagnostic program is no better than the intervention and follow-up care that it provides. To assure the rights of the at-risk child and help him get the services he needs, programs must provide an individual advocate for each child. Far too often children are screened and diagnosed but never receive any treatment because they are lost in the system. Our willingness to provide massive screening and follow-up intervention reflects the value our culture places on individual children and their right to an equal opportunity in development.

Some cities and states are revising their laws and assuming responsibility for educational programs that provide services for special needs children. One example of this is Massachusetts' Chapter 766 Special Education Law. This law provides for "finding" and evaluating children with special learning needs. While it does not screen all children, it does provide for screening and diagnostics for children whose parents and/or teachers request it. When screening indicates a problem, a comprehensive evaluation is undertaken by a team of professionals (medical, special education, psychology, social worker, speech and hearing, etc.). This team plans a "tailored" educational plan to meet the child's special learning needs. The parents must be satisfied with the plan or they can request a second analysis. The school then provides the services and monitors the plan's effectiveness periodically. This law is based on the assumption that all children have the legal right to an education that meets their needs.

The main problem with the Chapter 766 law is that it is very expensive and some people feel that it is not economically feasible for public schools to provide these services. There is clearly a need for more efficient ways to implement these services, as well as a need for everyone to evaluate his own commitment to providing every child with the opportunity for normal growth and development.

Conclusions

Testing children under 6 years of age is different than testing older children and requires special training and procedures. Psychological tests are systematic measures of behaviors that can be used to determine a child's rate of development and identify those at risk for difficulties. Tests for young children must always be administered individually to attain their optimum performance. The development and use of psychological tests suggest that a single index of intelligence or development is insufficient and can be misleading for diagnostic decisions and educational planning. Tests can range from behavioral measures that yield scores to tests of 1-day-old infants. Examiners must be aware of the special problems involved in testing young children and allow for limitations in both reliability and validity when interpreting results. All children should have developmental screening at or before the age of 3 to identify those at risk for future learning problems. No child should be given a diagnostic psychological test unless a specific problem is indicated. The "at risk" child should be evaluated and recommended for more comprehensive testing when necessary. Based on the testing results an educational program should be planned and implemented to meet the child's special learning needs. No testing procedure is any better than the follow-up treatment services that are provided.

REFERENCES

Anastasi, Anne. *Psychological Testing,* 3rd Ed. New York: MacMillan, 1968. A review of available individual and group tests with emphasis on principles of test construction.

Bayley, Nancy. *Bayley Scales of Infant Development: Manual.* New York: The Psychological Corp., 1969.

Beery, Keith. *Developmental Test of Visual-Motor Integration: Manual.* Chicago: Follett Publishing Co., 1967.

Boyd, R. D. *CCD Developmental Progress Scale.* Experimental form, manual and directions, June 1969.

Brazelton, T. B. "Neonatal Behavioral Assessment Scale." *National Spastics Society Monographs,* London: William Heineman and Son, 1973. A test manual.

Cattell, P. *The Measurement of Intelligence of Infants and Young Children.* New York: The Psychological Corp., 1940. A test manual.

Cronbach, Lee J. *Essentials of Psychological Testing.* 3rd Ed. New York: Harper, 1974. A review of psychological tests with emphasis on current statistical and empirical data.

Doll, E. A. *Vineland Social Maturity Scales.* Circle Pines, Minn.: American Guidance Service, Inc., 1965. A test manual.

Erikson, M. T., Johnson, N. M. and Campbell, F. A. "Relationships among Scores of Infant Tests for Children with Developmental Problems." *American Journal of Mental Deficiency,* July 1970, Vol. 75, pp. 102-104.

Frankenburg, W. and Dobbs, J. "The Denver Developmental Screening Test." *Journal of Pediatrics,* 1967, Vol. 71, p. 181.

Friedlander, B. Z., Sterrit, G. M., and Kirk, G. E. (Editors). *Exceptional Infant: Assessment and Intervention, Volume 3.* New York: Brunner/Mazel Inc., 1975. A current resource for research in testing and intervention with young children.

Gianni, M., *et al.* "The Rapid Developmental Screening Checklist." *American Academy of Pediatrics,* New York, February 1972.

Haynes, U. *A Developmental Approach to Casefinding with Special Reference to Cerebral Palsy, Mental Retardation, and Related Disorders.* Washington, D. C.: Government Printing Office, 1967. Source for the *Guide to Normal Milestones of Development.*

Knoblock, Hilda and Passamanick, Benjamin. *Gesell and Amatruda's Developmental Diagnosis.* 3rd Ed. New York: Harper and Row, 1974. A textbook of developmental evaluations for infants and preschoolers designed primarily for medical use.

Lewis, Michael (Ed.). *Origins of Intelligence.* New York: Plenum Press, 1976. A review of the concept of infant intelligence and the use of infant tests.

Meir, John. *Screening and Assessment of Young Children at Developmental Risk.* Washington, D. C.: DHEW Publication No. (05) 73-90. March 1973. A review of current screening instruments and relevant research findings.

Robb, G. P., Bernardoni, L. C., and Johnson, R. W. *Assessment of Individual Mental Ability.* Scranton, Pa.: Intext Educational Pub., 1972. A textbook that reviews the major individual intelligence tests and principles of administration.

Terman, Lewis and Merrill, Maud. *Stanford-Binet Intelligence Scale* (1972 Norms Edition). Boston: Houghton Mifflin Co., 1973. A test manual.

Uzgiris, Ina and Hunt, J. McVicer. *Assessment in Infancy.* University of Illinois Press, 1975. A manual and description of development of scale.

The research upon which the chapter is based was supported in part through the U.S. Department of Health, Education, and Welfare: Maternal and Child Health Service (Project 928).

III.

SPECIAL LEARNING PROBLEMS OF YOUNG CHILDREN

By Richard R. Schnell

Why do some children have more difficulty learning than others? During the past several years a new diagnostic catch-all, "learning disability" has been created to account for much of this phenomenon. Often there are disagreements about who these children are and how they got that way. Nevertheless, the label of learning disability is now very much in vogue. Unfortunately much of the recent attention has been directed at various diagnostic schemes and terminology. The children themselves are receiving less attention. For example, a controversy exists over whether most children who acquire the learning disability label are minimally brain damaged, that is, have a mild impairment in the functioning of the central nervous system which may result in learning problems. This dispute does not lead to an effective remediation program. It only deals with which professional group should be responsible. For example, if brain damage is present, the physician and not the educator is expected to assume responsibility for treatment and guidance.

But the majority of young children do not have significant learning problems, despite the fears stirred by floods of literature describing the many varieties of learning disabilities. Most children manifest expected individual learning differences. These normal differences in learning rates and styles have also added to the confusion. The concern with learning disabilities, however, has been helpful. It has required schools to adopt a more flexible and individualized approach to learning for all students.

But there remains a smaller group of young children who differ significantly from their peers in their learning. These children are by no means homogenous. To group them together does not suggest they have much in common except significant problems in acquiring new skills. Some of the children in this group have a "specific learning disability," one or more deficits, such as visual perception of symbols or word finding. Others in the group are mentally retarded, sensory handicapped, or emotionally disturbed. Indeed a number of the children have multiple problems, such as hearing impairments, emotional disturbances, or mental retardation with a specific learning disability. This chapter will provide an overview of many of the fundamental problems that affect the learning of young children and describe some of the programs that give assistance to them and their parents.

Labeling Children

In discussing children with learning handicaps, the emphasis will be on general groupings arranged according to their probable causes, rather than an extensive classification system and terminology. Labeling is fraught with problems. As Nicholas Hobbs indicates in his excellent book on the classification and labeling of children, "Classification can profoundly affect what happens to a child. It can open doors to service and experiences the child needs to grow in competence, to become a person sure of his worth and appreciative of the worth of others, to live with zest and to know joy. On the other hand, classification, or inappropriate classification, or failure to get needed classification—and the consequences that ensue—can blight the life of a child, reducing opportunity, diminishing his competence and self esteem, alienating him from others, nurturing a meanness of spirit, and making him less a person than he would become." Classification can serve to stigmatize children as deviant and create barriers between them and others.

Whether a child is normal or deviant is culturally determined by a particular society at a particular time and for a particular purpose. Howard Becker described the process as follows:

> Social groups create deviance by making rules whose infraction constitutes deviance, and by applying these rules to particular people and labeling them as outsiders...The deviant is one to whom the label has been successfully applied; deviant behavior is behavior that people so label.

Thus behavior of children who are mentally retarded, emotionally disturbed, or have physical disabilities can be placed on a continuum from very deviant to within normal expectations, depending upon the predominant views of the society. A child in our society is thought to be deviant if he is not trying to surpass his peers. But in a culture like that of the Zuni Indians of the Southwest, children have been taught not to excel at the expense of their peers. A Zuni child who consistently bettered his peers in an activity would be labeled as deviant.

Although labeling can often lead to negative consequences, it is essential in order to obtain services for groups of children, plan and organize programs for them, and determine outcomes of intervention efforts. A more fruitful procedure might scrutinize children's needs rather than their deficits. Nicholas Hobbs recommends a shift away from a focus on handicapped children per se, and toward what he refers to as an "ecological strategy," that is, on the family atmosphere to keep the handicapped child in as near-to-normal a setting as possible.

Mental Retardation

Over a decade ago Rick Heber commented that historically, mental retardation was a social, administrative, and legal concept, rather than a scientific one. How we decide who is mentally retarded depends mainly upon our interests and purpose. As Jane Mercer in her book *Labeling the Mentally Retarded* notes, "The perspective from which human behavior is viewed determines its meaning. What things are called and where the line is drawn between one class of things and another is socially arbitrated and validated through common usage."

Traditionally, mental retardation has been determined by measured performance on intelligence tests: an IQ score which is one or more standard deviations (usually 15 or 16 points) below the population mean (100). There is, however, a continuing controversy about the nature of intelligence, its organization, its predictability, its measurement, and its susceptibility to change. In 1958 the American Association on Mental Deficiency in its manual on terminology and classification emphasized that an IQ score should not be the sole criterion for retardation. The A.A.M.D. stated that, "Mental retardation refers to subaverage general intellectual functioning which originates during the developmental period and is associated with impairment in adaptive behavior." Adaptive behavior refers to an individual's effectiveness in coping with the demands of the environment. This emphasis on adaptive behavior precludes total reliance on the IQ score. The IQ score alone is inadequate. It cannot provide a description of how individuals operate at daily living tasks, or how they meet the expectations of their environment. The practice of attempting to predict future behavior from a single score in childhood can result in a self-fulfilling prophecy. Some children treated as retarded become retarded. Children who are classified as mentally retarded are as individually distinctive and statistically variable as children whose intelligence is within the average range and whose adaptive behavior is adequate for their circumstances.

Children have usually been labeled retarded because of their actual or anticipated difficulties in learning the skills that are important in the academic setting. Preschool children who are behind their age group in attaining developmental milestones such as walking and use of language become suspects for retardation. If psychological testing confirms deficient learning, in the absence of any important physical or environmental handicap, the child is eligible for the label of mental retardation. The American Association on Mental Deficiency describes five levels of retardation, each including a range of one standard deviation within a normal distribution of IQ scores. (See Figure 3.)

Excluding the borderline designation that identifies a group that may have some school related problems but whose members usually can maintain adequate adaptive behavior similar to their peers with higher IQ scores, about 3 percent of the total population of the United States is estimated to be mentally retarded. Many of the children who are described as mildly retarded will become relatively self sufficient with training. Children in the moderate group and below can learn simple skills but most will require a life-long sheltered environment.

Investigators have, however, consistently indicated that the highest incidence of mental retardation is reported during the school years (ages 5-18). Dramatically reduced numbers prevail at both pre- and post-school levels. The lower incidence for pre-school children occurs because mild delays are often not considered important by parents or others. But upon entering school these young children have difficulty with the curriculum. Similarly, many people who were designated as retarded during school years are able to maintain a job and live independently.

Children can fall into the retarded category for three major reasons. Statistically, intelligence is expected to fit a normal distribution with some children brighter than others. Just as we expect a few geniuses, we also expect a few profoundly retarded children. In a normal population some children will fall in the mentally retarded range. There are too many children in the retarded group, however, to be accounted for by this assumption alone. A second category of children are thought to be mentally retarded because of problems in central nervous system functioning resulting from such factors as genetics, nutrition, disease, or trauma. Brain damage or malfunction does not automatically produce mental retardation. It depends upon the location, degree, and timing of the problem. The so-called "disadvantaged" children make up the third category. Children in this group tend to be lower-class and minority children who do not have the same experiential background as their middle-class peers. Whether this difference in experience, which many

FIGURE 3. RETARDATION GROUPINGS

LEVEL	STANDARD DEVIATION UNITS BELOW THE POPULATION MEAN	APPROXIMATE PERCENTAGE OF THE MENTALLY RETARDED POPULATION
Borderline	1 to 2	Not Usually Considered Retarded
Mild	2 to 3	89 percent
Moderate	3 to 4	6 percent
Severe	4 to 5	3 ½ percent
Profound	5 or more	1 ½ percent

define as cultural, constitutes the only difference in children who obtain higher scores on intelligence tests is an issue of hot debate. Also, lower-class children may suffer central nervous system damage due to poor nutrition—both during and after pregnancy—inadequate health care, and greater exposure to disease and health hazards. Additionally, some children with severe emotional problems, sensory deficits, or specific learning disabilities are inappropriately designated as retarded.

Nature-Nurture Dispute

Recent research in both the biomedical and behavioral sciences demonstrates that both intellectual and biological development begin early in the life of a child and proceed with great rapidity for the first five years. During these years the child is vulnerable to developmental learning deficits stemming from genetic and/or environmental factors.

The learning-handicapped child has provided a battleground for those who see behavior as predominantly the result of genetic factors, as opposed to others who view behavior as the direct result of environmental influences. The emerging discipline of sociobiology takes the stand that all behavior has a firm biologic and genetic base, while some learning theorists emphasize learning experiences as central to all behavior.

Most behavior is co-determined by genetic factors and environmental experience. To assign weights to each is beyond the realm of this chapter. Both genetic determinants and environmental factors can interact to alleviate or accentuate the extent of a learning handicap.

A child's culture is an important contributing factor to the general environment. It's therefore heavily responsible for what we define as learning problems. Michael Cole and his colleagues have investigated cultural effects upon learning. They compared American students and Kpelle tribal members on numerous measures at various age levels. On some tasks the Kpelle tribal members were significantly less proficient, but on others they were clearly superior to their American counterparts. The results supported the hypothesis of Cole and his group that, "People will be good at things that are important to them and that they have occasion to do often." What our society decides is important for children to learn can be very different from that of another society. What constitutes a learning handicap will differ from culture to culture. It has been suggested that reading and writing disturbances may be different in varying languages depending upon whether the ideographic principle of writing is used (Chinese) instead of the conventional graphic signs (English). The remainder of this chapter will be devoted to describing the major causes of learning handicaps and some of the means of prevention and remediation.

Genetic Factors

The development of a child is the result of the interplay between his or her genetic composition and environment. Each child inherits 23 chromosomes, including one sex chromosome, from each parent, for a total of 46. A special pair of the 46 chromosomes are called the sex chromosomes because they determine the sex of the child. If the child receives a Y chromosome he will be male; if no Y chromosome is present, the child will have two X chromosomes and be female. On each chromosome are over a thousand genes which are so minute many have yet to be localized and identified. These genes carry the coded messages for the development of many of our traits, such as eye color, enzyme systems, and blood groups. These traits are the results of actions of single pairs of genes; one gene of the pair is obtained from each parent. If one of the genes in a pair controls the expression of a trait it is said to be "dominant." For example, the gene for brown eyes is dominant over the gene for blue eyes. A pair comprised of each gene will produce a brown eyed child. The other gene in the pair is said to be "recessive" in that it takes a pair of genes exactly alike to produce that trait. For example, both genes for blue eyes must be present to produce a blue eyed child. Some traits like height, weight, or intelligence are the result of the activities of multiple gene pairs and are described as polygenetic traits. The majority of genetic disorders appear to have a polygenic origin.

There are numerous genetic disorders which contribute to learning deficiencies. Extra or deficient chromosome material can be harmful, although the majority of fetuses with chromosomal aberrations are discarded prenatally as spontaneous abortions or still births. The most prevalent chromosomal problem (1 in 600 births) is Down syndrome (Mongolism) caused by an excess of chromosomal material. The most common type of Down syndrome occurs when an extra chromosome develops, making the total number of chromosomes 47, instead of the normal 46. Distinct physical characteristics, usually described as multiple congenital anomalies, of the face, hands, and sometimes of the cardiovascular system are associated with Down syndrome.

Children with Down syndrome frequently have some degree of mental retardation. Because of similar physical characteristics, many children with Down syndrome have been grouped together as look-alikes. But children with Down syndrome are not carbon copies of each other. Intelligence also varies with ability ranging from severe retardation to the average range, with the median score falling between the mild to moderate range of retardation. Efforts at early stimulation to encourage the maximum development of children with Down syndrome appear to be very encouraging.

A condition in which one sex chromosome is missing and one X chromosome is present is called Turner syndrome. Affected children will look like girls, and have been reported to have a very specific learning deficit in perceptual organization, although few are mentally retarded. This is the only specific learning disability that has been traced to a particular chromosome.

Recessive conditions not associated with sex chromosomes give rise to a number of potentially troubling situations. A group of recessive disorders which result in the deficiency of a particular enzyme system are known as inborn errors of metabolism. PKU (phenylketonuria) is one of the conditions which is routinely screened for at birth in most states. PKU is transmitted via a pair of recessive genes, one received from each parent, which results in a deficiency in a specific enzyme (phenylalanine hydroxylase) whose function is to metabolize an amino acid (phenylalanine) present in many foods like milk and meat. If children who have this condition are not put on special diets that reduce the amount of phenylalanine intake, many of them become irreversibly retarded. With an appropriate diet many of the children will not become retarded, although a number of children who have PKU will also have some school problems. How much of these problems are determined by PKU and how much by the effects of special diet is difficult to determine.

Other recessive conditions for which there are no treatments include disorders in the way the body handles fatty materials, such as Tay-Sachs and Niemann-Pick disease. Disorders of this type result in children who appear normal at birth and may even develop normally for a time. But they eventually begin to exhibit progressive retardation and neurological impairment that results in death during childhood.

Genetic counseling for parents with a family history of genetic problems can help parents evaluate the risk of having a child with a genetic disorder. Furthermore, pregnancies can be monitored for certain genetic diseases such as chromosomal errors and inborn errors of metabolism. This is done by a process called amniocentesis. A sample of amniotic fluid (the fluid surrounding the fetus) is drawn and cells from the fetus in the fluid are cultured. From these cell cultures the chromosomes can be examined and the presence or absence of certain enzymes detected. If an abnormal fetus is detected a therapeutic abortion may be elected by the parents.

Maternal Factors

The health of the mother throughout pregnancy affects the developing fetus. Lower class mothers, whose medical care and nutrition are poor, often give birth to premature or "small-for-dates" infants; those born at full term but weighing less than five pounds. Premature and small-for-dates infants may develop more significant disabilities than those born at full term and weighing above five pounds. Women who are heavy smokers throughout their pregnancy, as well as mothers addicted to heroin or alcohol also tend to have low birth weight babies.

Considerable research indicates that malnutrition affects the developing brain both during pregnancy and early childhood. It is not yet clear how much of the impairment is irreversible. Stronger measures to eliminate malnutrition from all levels of society and at all ages, particularly during pregnancy and early childhood, are obviously needed.

During pregnancy the fetus is susceptible to damage through exposure of the mother to such forces as radiation and physical trauma, as well as certain drugs, hormones and infections passed through the placenta. The increased birth rate of physically handicapped children in Europe caused by mothers taking the anti-nausea drug thalidomide is an example. Rubella (German measles) has been an important threat to the fetus in past years. A nation wide program of inoculating children against rubella has substantially reduced the incidence of this disease. A woman in her first five months of pregnancy who contracted rubella could pass the virus on to her fetus. Congential rubella can result in severe fetal damage, ranging from death of the fetus to heart defects, physical handicaps, retardation, behavioral anomalies, and/or sensory deficits. The 1964 epidemic of rubella in the United States produced an estimated 20,000 children with congenital malformations.

Rh blood factor incompatibility between mother (Rh-negative) and fetus (Rh-positive) can result in damage to the fetus. The transfer from the mother of antibodies that act against Rh-positive fetal red blood cells in the fetus can impair the development of the fetal central nervous system which may lead to retardation. A technique for intrauterine exchange transfusions of Rh-positive blood to the fetus also makes it possible to counteract adverse influences on the fetus during pregnancy.

Birth and Infancy Factors

Traumatic events, both before and after birth, can have a disproportionately greater influence than similar events occuring later in life. Because the trauma affects a developing central nervous system, the effects tend to be generalized and often irreversible. Early damage is significant, but later experiences can also be important. Hilda Knobloch and Benjamin Pasamanick call this the "continuum of reproductive casualty." Early damage can influence sensorimotor or cognitive development, which may predispose a child to later psychological deficits ranging from retardation to specific learning disabilities.

Damage to the baby during birth can occur for a number of reasons, including a prolonged and difficult delivery, prematurity, toxemia, hemorrhage, and infection. Administration of drugs to the mother and operative complications at the time of delivery can also harm the baby. A large group of children who develop motor deficits as the result of damage at birth have been designated as children with cerebral palsy. All of these children share a disorder of motor development, but these disorders fall along a continuum from severe to very minor problems of motor development, and may be associated with additional handicaps such as mental retardation or specific learning disabilities.

Otto Rank suggested in 1929 that the trauma of birth is responsible for the development of anxiety in the child. This view has never been substantiated but a number of other investigators have supported the notion of birth as a traumatic experience because of the techniques employed at the time of delivery. In 1975, Frederick Leboyer, a French obstetrician, described the emotions and sensations of the baby as it is born and immediately after birth. He criticized some of the usual obstetrical procedures because he felt they interfered with the normal birth process. Although his claims for future influences on the emotional development of the child have yet to be demonstrated, many of the delivery techniques he advocates are used routinely in the Netherlands which has a markedly lower infant mortality rate than the United States.

As previously discussed, adequate birth weight is extremely important for the well being of the new born. Infants born prematurely or lighter than five pounds may suffer a host of developmental problems including specific learning disabilities. Retrospective studies of children with learning disabilities frequently discover prematurity and anoxia. Anoxia is oxygen deprivation to the baby during birth, a condition that could result in brain damage. A study of 7-year-old children who had suffered anoxia at birth found that some of the children were not retarded, but appeared to have specific learning deficits. They demonstrated a deficit in abstract ability and did more poorly on a test of perceptual-motor functioning.

Childhood diseases can also result in learning problems. Infections that affect the developing brain of the young child (encephalitis and meningitis) can produce impaired learning ability. These infections occur either as a specific disease or as the result of another infection, such as measles. Antibiotics have helped in the treatment of bacterial infections but viral infections remain difficult to treat. The Center for Disease Control estimates that there are approximately 39,000 cases of bacterial meningitis per year. The age of greatest risk is 6 to 12 months, with 90 percent of the cases occurring between 1 month to 5 years.

Due to its recent notoriety, lead poisoning is a condition on which an appreciable amount of data has been collected. Chronic lead poisoning is more common in slum housing. Young children ingest lead by licking, gnawing or eating substances that contain lead, typically flakes of lead based paint. Continued ingestion of lead can produce medical problems leading to specific learning disabilities. If the poisoning is more severe, retardation and death can result. Treatment techniques are available, but to be maximally effective they must be administered before the child has ingested significant quantities of lead. Lead poisoning is an entirely preventable disorder, requiring only that children not be exposed to lead; yet it continues to be a problem, particularly among the poor.

The integrity of a child's sensory development is another important variable contributing to learning. Although few children are totally blind or deaf, they may have a visual or auditory impairment which can interfere with normal learning. Visual impairment can lead to difficulties in motor development, while a hearing loss can inhibit language development. Screening for visual and auditory defects in infancy is now possible and children with these disabilities can receive treatment and stimulation. The child with both auditory and visual handicaps remains one of the most difficult to design adequate programs for. These defects must be discovered early if the child's developmental course is to progress smoothly.

Emotional and Social Factors

Abused or battered chidren often begin life without handicaps, but subsequently exhibit problems that interfere with learning. These children may suffer from drastic physical abuse or forms of mistreatment such as neglect, excessive pressure, and ridicule. Reasons for the abuses are multidimensional, relating to ethnic group, social class, ability to tolerate stress, intellectual level, and emotional adjustment. Characteristics of the child who is prone to abuse are less well known. Children who appear violent and express this through frequent temper tantrums at an early age are more likely to suffer various forms of abuse.

Emotional concerns of young children are capable of interfering with learning processes. Problems of an emotional nature concern all children from time to time in early childhood, but if they are more than temporary they can interfere with the learning of basic skills necessary for future learning. Because early development progresses at a rapid rate, there are many opportunities for maladaption. Emotional concerns can lead to maladaptive behavior; behavior which affects a child's capacity to deal with his environment, as well as his capacity to learn. Whether the behavior problem persists often depends upon the nature of the problem and the environment in which the child is living. A change in environmental circumstances can often positively influence behavior. Some changes may be difficult to accomplish, however, because they can involve important changes in the perception and behavior of the child's family. The child's family must be motivated for such a change. Many of the relatively simple problems of early childhood, although troubling at the time, do not affect later development.

The first problem areas of early childhood usually center around the child's predominant activities of sleeping, eating, crying and elimination. Early childhood can be marked by frustration and conflict over these issues. The young child is very dependent, but wants to have his own way. He develops strong emotions, but is expected to control them. He has a strong need to explore the environment, but has to be protected from injury. His social development is related to his success in attending to what others are saying and doing, and his skills at expressing his own thoughts and feelings. Children with handicaps, especially those involving the communication process, are more likely to develop maladaptive behavior. The reactions of others to a child's handicap will partially determine the child's self-concept, and thus influence his future behavior. The child, although aware of his limitations, should develop a realistic picture of his capabilities and be able to maximize his personal effectiveness.

The most severe emotional problems are those that significantly impair the learning capabilities of the child over an extended period of time. The most oppressive of these conditions are the childhood psychoses of schizophrenia and autism. Childhood schizophrenia has been difficult to define and its recognition as a distinct entity has been problematical. It is thought by some to be a condition in which a child, after a relatively normal period of development, begins to regress; withdraw from interpersonal relationships and have difficulty discerning what is real from what is not. This pattern is usually accompanied by an increase in behavior inappropriate for the child's circumstances.

Autism has received more attention, but many problems still remain in considering it as a separate syndrome. Two important recurring diagnostic features in autism are extreme and sustained impairment of emotional relationships with people, and preoccupation with particular objects. Early research on childhood psychosis emphasized the environment, especially the mother, as the cause. The pendulum now seems to be swinging back in the direction of biological and genetic factors as being of greater importance.

Diagnosticians have often attempted to demonstrate that although psychotic children may be functioning at a retarded intellectual level they have potential for average or above intelligence. The diagnosticians have demonstrated this by searching for islands of intellectual competence in the child's behavior. Unfortunately this exercise frequently takes the form of determining whether a child is worth treating or not. There are no universally successful treatment techniques for psychotic children, but many mental health workers seem to feel that psychosis is more worthy of treatment if the child will not become retarded. As a result, there are large numbers of seriously disturbed children in the country for whom there are few services and treatment.

Specific Learning Disabilities

Even with adequate vision, hearing, and intelligence, a child may have a specific learning deficit that can lead to difficulty in language development and/or the attainment of perceptual-motor skills. This does not mean that children with other problems, be they sensory defects, mental retardation, physical handicaps, or emotional concern, cannot have specific learning disabilities. The myth that only children of average or above intelligence have specific learning disabilities seems to be fueled by the hope that learning disabilities will be seen as a more socially acceptable kind of deviancy than any other.

Some of the classification schemes developed to describe these deficits borrow heavily on neurological terminology, and attempt to use concepts applicable to adults that cannot be applied to the growing child. Parents as well sometimes mistakenly treat their young children as miniature adults, even though children's thought processes and feelings are a long way from the adult level. Adult neurological problems are imposed on a developed central nervous system. Similar problems in childhood interact with a developing central nervous system, and often produce very different results. For example, the concept of aphasia has been very helpful in describing adults who have lost expressive language skills. But it is less useful in describing why some children fail to develop expressive language. Physicians, particularly neurologists, have frequently been looked to by educators and parents to supply an effective understanding and treatment of learning disabilities. But they sometimes just apply a medical label to the problem and offer tentative explanations without formulating a meaningful learning program for the child. Terms with a more descriptive and developmental base are more useful than medical labels. Such terms can more readily lead to a pragmatic understanding. They are more helpful in formulating a learning program that can be carried on in the home and eventually in the school.

To better understand some of the specific learning disabilities we can think of the nervous system as a computer. The nervous system has three important functions. (1) Input information is received through a sensory organ, recognized by the system as information, and decoded. (2) The information is then organized; some of it is integrated with already present information, some of it is stored in memory, and some of it may call for the retrieval of other information already stored in memory. (3) The information may then result in an output expression such as movement or verbal utterances. The common kinds of information processed by the system involve vision, hearing, and touch. Children may have problems in dealing with specific kinds of information at any or all steps in the system.

A child with normal hearing may have difficulty in understanding what is said to him, that is, a deficit in auditory receptive language. This deficit may result from difficulty in discrimination between the sounds of words or in processing the sounds heard. Such a child may respond appropriately when *shown* what to do. But oral directions, especially as they become more complex, may confuse the child. Communicating with a child who has this deficit can be a frustrating experience for a parent.

Other children may have no problem detecting and understanding the spoken word, but have trouble organizing a response. Doris Johnson and Helmer Myklebust describe three groups of disturbances. The first group has a deficit in re-auditorization. The children can understand spoken words but cannot remember or retrieve them for spontaneous use. Another group of children has defective syntax. They can use single words and short phrases but cannot plan and organize words for the expression of ideas. Words are left out in sentences or get out of order. The third group of youngsters cannot produce the motor patterns necessary for speaking and thus have difficulty in learning to say words. This condition is often designated as apraxia. Apraxia is an inability to perform certain movements without paralysis or loss of sensation. Those afflicted cannot voluntarily initiate the movements of the tongue and lips necessary for the formation of spoken words.

A group of similar disorders exists for the visual realm. Given normal vision a child may not be able to discriminate between circles and squares. On another level, a child with adequate visual perception may not be able to imitate a circular motion in the air, or when asked to draw a circle may not be able to retrieve the concept from memory. Similar problems exist in the tactual realm, but have not been studied as thoroughly. There is a group of children who have come to attention because of their excessive response to being touched. These tactually defensive children do not like to be touched, because they have difficulty in telling where and how hard they have been touched.

A group of children who have attracted the most attention are those who have been called hyperactive or hyperkinetic. Children with this condition have been described as extremely active, unable to sit still or concentrate for more than a few seconds at a time, and frequently have sleep problems. When first described a drug treatment was devised which involved such stimulant drugs as ritalin and dexedrine, and, more recently, caffeine. The drugs produced the paradoxical effect of slowing the children down, enabling them to concentrate better. This drug program was not successful with all such children. Nevertheless, the development of a drug program coincided with a greatly increased number of hyperkinetic children found by schools. Closer inspection determined that a number of the drug treated children were causing problems in school, but were not exhibiting the characteristics of hyperkinetic behavior. The appeal of drugs to control children's behavior in school was apparently too great to resist. The diagnostic issue of who really is hyperkinetic and who is not continues to be a problem. Children can be overactive at various times for many different reasons. The newest area of investigation is centering on the possible contribution food additives, and artificial colors and flavors, may make to hyperkinetic behavior.

Programs and Conclusions

Many things can be done to help potentially learning disabled youngsters. Despite the importance of biological and genetic factors, improvement in the environment can lead to positive changes in learning.

The classic study by Skeels and Dye in 1939, demonstrated significant changes in IQ score due to environmental manipulation. Infants from an orphanage who were given individual stimulation and attention improved their IQ score by an average of 28 points while children who were not stimulated lost an average of 26 points.

An often quoted long range study by Heber and Garber of families in an economically disadvantaged urban area initially found maternal intelligence as the best single predictor of low intelligence in their children. To investigate this phenomenon, a group of infants born to mothers whose IQ was 75 or below was studied. One goal of the program was to prevent mental retardation in the children by helping their mothers improve their employment potential, increase earnings, gain self confidence, and achieve better homemaking and childrearing skills. The other major goal has been to provide a direct intervention program for the children, beginning between 3 to 6 months of age and continuing until they have entered the first grade. Though not complete, the study has shown that at 5 years of age the children in the program are an average of 21 points higher in IQ than a group of similar children not in the program.

Other kinds of early intervention and stimulation programs that begin at the birth of a potentially handicapped child are also beginning to demonstrate their effectiveness, for example, the programs for children with Down syndrome cited earlier. The involvement and concern of the child's parents, relevant social agencies, and community is mandatory if the child is to be helped to function in our society. The last few years have seen a welcome change in our attitudes about where the handicapped belong. Most children with mild handicaps have always been able to live in normal society with their families. Large residential institutions, such as state training schools for mentally retarded invididuals and state hospitals for those designated as emotionally disturbed, have been used for the more seriously handicapped. Now there is a substantial movement to allow even the most seriously handicapped to live and function in normal society as much as they are able.

Programs can be devised to help children with actual or potential learning handicaps. The major need is to prevent the problem. Much can be done if our society will confront the major issues of poverty, discrimination, malnutrition, poor housing, inadequate health care, and poor educational opportunities.

REFERENCES

Cole, M., Gay J., Glich, J.A., and Sharp, D.W. *The Cultural Context of Learning and Thinking.* New York: Basic Books, 1971. This volume examines the relationship between culture, thinking and learning. To explore the effects of culture on behavior the authors have combined anthropological, linguistic, and psychological techniques in studying Kpelle tribal members and comparing them with American students.

Crisis in Child Mental Health: Challenge for the 1970s. Report on the Joint Commission
    for the Mental Health of Children. New York: Harper & Row, 1970. The report gives
    evidence of the inadequate services and programs that foster the mental health of
    children. The aspects of contemporary American society that affect growth and
    development are explored giving great importance to the earliest years of life. It also
    gives detail and specificity to recommendations about what should be done at national,
    state and local levels.

Environment, Heridity and Intelligence. Cambridge: Harvard Educational Review, 1969.
    The major article in this paperback reprint of articles appearing in the Harvard Educa-
    tional Review is by Arthur Jensen. In this article Jensen discusses the relative con-
    tributions of genetic and environmental influences on IQ taking the stand that genetic
    factors are the most important and thus disparaging the efforts of preschool programs
    for the disadvantaged. Following this article are rebuttals by six psychologists and a
    geneticist who present contrary evidence.

Friedlander, B.Z., Steritt, G.M., and Kirk, G.E. (Eds.) *Exceptional Infant: Assessment
    and Intervention.* Vol. 3. New York: Brunner/Mazel, 1975. Contained in this book is a
    collection of articles on recently developed assessment and intervention strategies with
    the exceptional infant. It provides an impressive discussion of attempts to increase the
    likelihood that children, even when seriously handicapped, will achieve more adequate
    use of their potential.

Hobbs, N. *The Futures of Children.* San Francisco: Jossey-Bass, 1975. The effects
    (beneficial as well as harmful) of classification and labeling on handicapped, disad-
    vantaged, and delinquent children and youth are explored in this book. How to
    diminish the stigmatizing effects of labeling is thoroughly discussed.

Stone, L.J., Smith, H.T., and Murphy, L.B. (Eds.) *The Competent Infant.* New York:
    Basic Books, 1973. This is a comprehensive compilation of recent research that focuses
    on development from the fetal stage to 15 months. Specific sections cover individuality
    in development, prenatal, and perinatal development, capabilities of the newborn,
    development during the first year, deprivations and enrichment of early experience,
    and the infant as a social being.

**The research upon which the chapter is based was supported in part
through the U.S. Department of Health, Education, and Welfare:
Maternal and Child Health Service (Project 928).**

IV.

BOY, GIRL, OR PERSON? Current Issues in Sex Role and Sex Identity

By William Kilpatrick

Sex identity at first glance appears to be a simple matter of boy/girl. It is, in fact, a most complicated phenomenon. Adult sex identify results from a mixture of genetic, hormonal, cultural, and psychological forces in proportions that are largely unknown. The scientific complexity of sex identify is matched by the emotional reaction it evokes. Sex identity is usually the first question that pops into everyone's mind whenever a new human being enters the world. Moreover, some of our best insights into the nature of sex identify come from studies of homosexuals, transexuals, and transvestites—sexual minorities that other people often react to with violent emotions. The sex roles that accompany sex identity are equally charged with emotions: few areas of controversy have touched so many nerves as has the topic of sex role liberation. Women complain that their role leads to drudgery and neurosis, while men grumble that their role leads to drudgery and ulcers. To complicate matters further there are difficult philosophical problems. Assuming that sex roles can be shifted, the question remains, "In what direction?" "What is the healthy self?" "What constitutes a meaningful life?"

This essay is not so much concerned with uncomplicating the problems of sex identity, as it is with placing them in some kind of perspective. The first order of business is to establish that differences do exist—boys and girls differ in their response pattern even in the first few weeks of life. Whether these differences are caused mainly by biology or mainly by culture will then be discussed. Some practical suggestions for encouraging masculinity in boys and femininity in girls will follow. Finally, this essay will address the question of roles. Should we attempt to raise girls to be more like boys? Should we raise boys to be more like girls? Or should we, in line with the currently fashionable thinking, just raise them both as "persons"? And, if we decide on this last course of action, what kind of a person do we want?

Sex Differences

So far, the new children don't appear to be any different from the old children with respect to sex differences. The discrepancies are still apparent. There are differences not only in anatomy and physical strength but also in perception, intellectual functioning, and exploratory behavior.

To begin with, males seem to be at a biological disadvantage. Although more males are conceived than females, more males are stillborn or spontaneously aborted. The rate of disease and mortality is also higher for males in childhood. Males have more genetically transmitted defects such as hemophilia and color blindness. Learning disorders are more frequent among males than females; so are behavior disorders. A higher percentage of males are mentally subnormal.

Males, however, tend to display more independent and exploratory behavior. Observation of infants at the Fels Research Institute indicates that even at 13 months girls are less adventurous, stay closer to their mother, are reluctant to leave her, and return to her for reassurance more often than boys. When a wire mesh barrier was used to block access to the mother, girls tended to cry and do nothing, while boys made attempts to get around the barier or push it aside.

A number of studies summarized by psychologist Eleanor Macoby show that girls have superior verbal ability, while boys excell at spatial tasks; boys have more analytic ability, while girls rely more on "circumstantial'' evidence or intuition when solving problems. Girls learn to count at an earlier age, but boys later surpass them in arithmetical reasoning. Other studies indicate that boys are less cooperative and more competitive than girls, and engage in more acts of aggression. This type of behavior is even observed in the kibbutz environment where radical attempts have been made to eliminate sex role typing.

Finally, it should be noted that some of these differences are manifested very early in life. Greater spatial ability has been found in boys as young as two weeks old; another study reveals that at 14 weeks girls are more responsive to auditory stimuli, while boys are more responsive to visual stimuli. (This may account for the fact that grown up boys are more easily aroused by visual pornography than are girls.)

It is clear then, that above and beyond the anatomical distinctions, there are several ways in which boys and girls differ. But where do these sex differences come from? Are children born with them? Or do they result from an early and all-pervasive cultural conditioning?

Biology vs. Culture

Hermaphrodites are individuals who are genetically of one sex but have the sex organs of the opposite sex. For example, a child may be born female (two X chromosomes) but may have the external genitals of a male. In such cases, a mistake in gender assignment might easily be made. A girl may be registered as a boy on the birth certificate, given a boy's name, and be brought up as a boy. Or a genetic boy may be brought up as a girl. If the mistake is discovered in time it is possible to reassign sex, administer hormonal treatments, and perform an operation to bring the physical appearance in line with the chromosonal reality. And all of this can be accomplished with no great harm to the child's emotional development provided that sufficient counseling is given to the parents.

However, there is a point beyond which the reassignment does not take hold or else takes hold poorly. Dr. John Money and his colleagues at the Johns Hopkins Hospital have been treating hermaphrodites for two decades. They conclude that there is a critical period for the learning of sex identity—and that period seems to commence about 18 months after birth and end at about 4 or 5 years of age. After 18 months, attempts to reassign sex may be resisted by the child who is developing or has already developed a sexual self-concept. After a while, the girl who is brought up as a boy comes to consider herself a boy, to act as a boy, to be treated as a boy by others. For all intents and purposes she is a boy. To attempt after 4 years or 14 years to convince her otherwise may result in grave psychological harm.

Such findings have been accepted in some quarters as incontrovertible evidence that sex identity and sex roles are mainly a matter of cultural conditioning. If you raise a girl as a boy you will produce a boy despite the genetic programming. In other words, cultures are more powerful than chromosomes. It is possible, however, to interpret the evidence so that biology emerges as the dominant factor. But before looking at that side of the coin let us first consider more of the data supporting the contention that our sexual nature is determined by our upbringing.

Occasionally, an individual who is anatomically normal will express a strong desire to be a member of the opposite sex. The desire may be so pressing that the individual requests or even demands an operation to change his or her sex. As far as the transsexual is concerned, the operation is for the sake of correcting a mistake of birth. Most transsexual men (a man who wishes to become a woman) claim that ever since their earliest years they sensed something was wrong. They felt themselves to be a girl who had somehow been born into the body of a boy.

At first glance the transsexual phenomenon would appear to fly in the face of the cultural argument, for these are people who are resisting enormous cultural pressure to conform, who are contemplating or have actually carried out a course of action that is appalling to a great many in our society. But, although they may ignore the larger culture, there is evidence that transsexuals do respond to the culture of the home during the period (18 months to 4 or 5 years) which Money identifies as critical for learning sex identity. Dr. Richard Green and Dr. Robert Stoller of the U.C.L.A. Medical School have both done extensive counseling with transsexuals, with feminine boys, and with masculine girls. Both have written books on the subject, and both concur that cross-sex interests and behavior result primarily from certain family patterns. For instance, Dr. Green lists the following factors as being associated with boyhood femininity:

(1)   Indifference of parents to feminine behavior in a boy. Typically, parents seem unconcerned when their son plays with dolls, or prefers to play at stewardess or nurse rather than pilot or doctor.

(2)   Parental encouragment of such behavior. Parents think it cute and amusing when their 4- or 5-year-old son dresses up in his mother's slip and applies mascara, rouge, and nail polish.

(3)   Frequent cross-dressing of a boy by a female. Dr. Green describes the case of a 3-year-old boy whose grandmother, in addition to dressing him as a girl, often polished his nails and curled his hair. Older sisters often play the same role.

(4)   Overprotection of a son by his mother, and inhibition of rough-and-tumble play. The mother of one 2-year-old would not allow the boy to accompany his father to the men's public bathroom. Typically, these chidren are discouraged from climbing, running, wrestling, even from riding tricycles.

(5) Excessive attention of mother to son; excessive physical contact between mother and son. Feminine boys tend to get a great deal of cuddling from their mothers. They may often sleep with their mothers—a practice which sometimes continues into adolescence. One boy, mentioned by Green, was so closely identified with his mother that he developed stomach aches whenever she had gall bladder symptoms.

(6) Rejection by the father, or absence of an older male as a model. Typically the father is uninvolved with his son in the early years, and then is disappointed with his son's lack of interest in masculine play.

(7) Physical beauty of a boy that prompts adults to treat him as a girl. Feminine boys often have a remarkable physical beauty, and are frequently mistaken for girls. By the age of 5 or 6 they may develop exaggerated feminine hand mannerisms, hip swing, even an effeminate lisp.

(8) A relative lack of male playmates during the boy's early socialization period. Either there are no boys available to play with or the boy prefers to play with girls. The teasing which feminine boys receive from other boys when they start school reinforces this pattern.

(9) A dominant mother and a powerless father. This is evident in the transcripts of interviews between Dr. Green and the parents of feminine boys. Mother to father: "Why don't you tell Dr. Green what you're concerned about?" She is not satisfied with his answer. Mother to father again: "Yes, but you're concerned really about him being *feminine,* aren't you?" This patronizing attitude continues throughout the interview.

(10) Castration anxiety. When dressing up in female clothing, many 4- and 5-year-old feminine boys experience erections often accompanied by some degree of anxiety. This may be interpreted as a form of castration anxiety.

Once again, these studies lend support to the notion that sex identity is learned either from culture or family, or both in conjunction. In its more familiar form the argument goes like this: boys gain a masculine identity because we dress them in blue, give them trucks to play with, encourage independence and discourage shows of emotion; girls gain a feminine identity because we dress them in pink, give them dolls to play with, and encourage nurturance and passivity. A corollary of this position is that sex identity is malleable, that biology has little to do with it, and that sex roles can be changed by changing cultural expectations. In short, if you treat a boy in a feminine way he will develop feminine characteristics.

There are problems with this argument, however. For instance, many of the feminine boys cited in Green's study grew up to a masculine, heterosexual identity despite their early conditioning. Moreover, the possibility exists that biological factors predisposed the parents to provide a feminine conditioning: the physical beauty of these boys certainly influenced the response to them; had they been husky and mannish looking, the thought of dressing them as girls might not have occurred to anyone. There also exists the possibility that these boys had a lower level of androgenic hormones. These hormones govern the development of male sex characteristics (such as body hair) and seem also to be related to aggression and competition. Boys with a lower level of androgen would therefore tend to have a lower level of aggressiveness. Consequently they would tend to avoid rough play, and prefer the company of girls; and consequently their mothers would respond to them in a protective way.

If one takes a closer look at the data, it becomes clear that biology cannot easily be pushed aside. Consider again the studies of hermaphrodites. The hermaphroditic condition is brought about prenatally by excesses, deficiencies, or errors of the hormones which govern the development of sex organs. For example, a genetic female who is exposed to extra androgens in the womb (either as a result of an hereditary problem in the adrenal glands or as an accidental side effect of drugs given to the mother during pregnancy) may be born with an enlarged clitoris which is mistaken for a penis. We have already noted how great a power the culture can exert in such cases of mistaken identity. However, it is well to remember that in these cases the biological forces are at odds. Chromosomes pull in one direction while hormones and physical appearance pull in the other. It's a divide and conquer situation in which the forces of biology are in disarray while the forces of culture have the field. In normal development chromosomes, hormones, and physical appearance act to reinforce each other so that the influence of culture is considerably less potent.

Of particular interest are those cases where females become androgenized (masculinized) in the womb but not to the extent that a mistake in gender identity is made. Yet these genetic females who are given an ordinary female upbringing turn out to be far more masculine in their behavior and interests when compared with normal girls. In a study done by Money and Anke Ehrhardt the androgenized girls were found to be much more interested in rough play, athletics, boys' clothes and toys, more prone to fighting and other tomboy behavior, and much less interested in dolls and houseplay. In addition they were much more likely to think in terms of future careers rather than in terms of marriage and motherhood.

Further evidence of the biological basis of sex identity can be found in experimental studies of animals. In one study where baby monkeys were separated from their parents at birth, it was observed that within a matter of weeks the male monkeys spontaneously began to exhibit aggressive, rough-and-tumble behavior, while the female monkeys spontaneously exhibited passive and nurturing behavior. Obviously this sex differentiated behavior cannot be explained in terms of cultural conditioning since these monkeys had been deprived of their "culture": there were no models of masculinity or femininity for them to imitate. In other experiments with primates it has been demonstrated that aggressiveness is linked with the level of *testosterone,* the chief androgenic or male hormone. Not only is it possible to reverse the dominance order in the male monkeys by injecting the low-ranking monkeys with testosterone, but it is also possible to create dramatic aggressive behavior in female monkeys by the prenatal administration of male hormones.

There is further evidence that mental processes are affected by sex hormones. It has been observed, for instance, that boys with certain types of endocrine disorders display lower spatial and numerical ability than normal boys, but have greater verbal ability. And Money and his colleagues have observed a trend toward high IQ in females exposed to an excess of androgens prior to birth. Such findings have forced Dr. Money to retreat somewhat from his earlier culturist position to the point where he concedes that sex hormones influence pathways in the central nervous system which, in turn, determine many of the differences between male and female behavior.

But for parents and others concerned with raising young children the crucial question is not whether biology has the main say in determining sex identity or whether culture does. A more important question for them is, "When does the critical period arrive and when does it depart?" The answer is that it comes earlier and departs sooner than most people realize. Dr. Green in his study on feminine boys found that their enduring interest in wearing girls' clothes most frequently had its onset between the second and third birthday. Yet most parents tended to ignore this early behavior and only showed concern when the practice continued into the school years. Dr. Green writes, "The age at which most parents consider male and female gender identity to be *emerging* is essentially when it has already established *rigid footing.*" What parents consider to be "just a stage" is actually the crucial period for the fixing of sex identity. The years between 2 and 4 which are critical for acquiring language are also the salient years for acquiring one's sexual identity.

Psychological Considerations

It should be obvious at this point that sex identity results from a complicated mix of culture and biology. It may be more useful, however, to discuss sex identity not as a biological thrust or as a cultural imperative but as a psychological need. To complicate the problem a bit let us consider some additional facts—facts that cannot be so easily explained in purely biological or cultural terms. It is interesting to note, for example, that family patterns similar to those which produce feminine boys frequently produce aggressive, acting-out delinquents. Consider also the fact that there are many more males than females who become transsexuals or homosexuals. Males, in general seem to have more difficulty in establishing a sex identity than do females. Why should that be? And if it is true, why do females seem less happy than males with their sex roles?

One explanation, put forward by sociologist David Lynn, is that both boys and girls start off with a feminine identification because the earliest and most formative experiences of both are with the mother while the father tends to be an absent or shadowy figure. The father, even when he is home, leaves most of the intimate child raising activities to the mother. She bathes, feeds, and puts to bed. The child follows her through her round of household activities but has only the vaguest notion of what the father does. So for boys as well as girls the first object of identification is the mother; the most readily available model of sex identity is a feminine one. A typical illustration is the boy whose father had just returned from a long tour of duty in Vietnam. The father, in an effort to re-establish a male bond with his 4-year-old son, invited the boy to watch him shave. He was caught off guard, however, when the boy, who had already developed his own notions about shaving, began applying shaving cream to his legs.

This early identification with the mother is fine for the girl but sooner or later the boy is expected to repent his error and make a male identification. This means that much of his early sex identification has to be undone. He must switch off one track and onto another. Unfortunately, some boys get derailed in the process. Many boys are so thoroughly identified with their mothers that they are unable to make the switch. Even for those who do, the passage is often a rough one.

The strain which this transition entails may account for the fact that boys seem more insecure about their sex identity than do girls. Most boys and a good many men spend a lot of time and energy trying to prove that they really are masculine. What this compulsive need really proves, of course, is that there is something very fragile about the male ego. While females may be concerned with proving that they are attractive or desirable, they have comparatively little need to prove that they are, in fact, females. The Lynn thesis would account, moreover, for the fact that about four or five times as many males as females wish to change their sex. It could also account for the greater incidence of homosexuality among males. It would account for the fact that most boys go through a period of "girl hating" during which they seem to renounce their former feminine identification and all the "girlish" things that went with it. They make up for their past "mistake", the error of their youth, by ostracizing girls, or teasing them, or pulling their hair—anything which will prove that they are no longer among the number of girls. This is fairly common behavior among grammar school children, but parents and teachers who observe extremes of this anti-girl rowdyism may take it as a sign that such boys sorely need to have their sense of masculinity reinforced.

But if males are so insecure about their sex identity why do so many females struggle for liberation? To resolve this paradox it is necessary to make a distinction between sex identity and sex role. Sex identity is a conviction—partly unconscious—that one belongs to the sex one has been born into. A secure sexual identity is manifested as a feeling of comfortableness with one's masculinity or femininity. Sex roles, on the other hand, are composed of the various activities and opportunities which society (but also biology) assign to one sex or the other. Since the male role carries with it more privileges and prerogatives it is not unusual for females to be envious of it, and dissatisfied with the more limited scope of action afforded by the traditional female role. Yet the woman who is dissatisfied with her role may still feel content with her identity as a female. Conversely, the man who is relatively content with his role may suffer from a gnawing sense of insecurity over his manhood.

The hypothesis that males are less secure about their sex identity would help to explain another well known phenomenon. Men experience a great deal of difficulty in accepting or expressing the feminine side of their nature, while women may freely express many masculine attributes, such as wearing men's clothes or doing traditionally male work. Perhaps the woman's greater flexibility is an index of a more secure sexual identity. In any event it would seem logical that an individual with a strong sense of personal identity would have less need to rely on society's definition of masculinity or femininity. One interesting implication of this theory is that a viable sex role liberation is most likely to be achieved by those who start off with a strong sense of either masculine or feminine identity.

Many societies have institutions which implicitly recognize the difficulty that males have in establishing sex identity. The primitive initiation rite for males can be seen as an attempt on the part of society to ratify a boy's transition from feminine to masculine identity. These rites of passage not only confirm adult status, they also confirm sex identity. Usually these rituals involve lengthy seclusion from women, circumcision ceremonies, and some ordeal or test of endurance. Paradoxically, the most severe initiation rites are to be found in societies where mother and son sleep together for the first few years of the boy's life and where the father is more or less kept out of the picture. A possible explanation for the harsh initiation rites in these child-indulgent societies is that they are necessary to help the boy break from his strong identification with the mother.

Rites of passage serve another function as well. They head off adolescent rebellion by admitting teenage boys to adult male status. The primitive wisdom behind this strategy is a recognition of the principle that society's most dangerous enemy is the "momma's boy." If this principle doesn't seem to make sense, consider what happens in societies which have no initiation rites, and yet have family patterns which involve absent fathers and exclusive mother-son relationships (the pattern for many families in the U.S.). True, such family situations often produce feminine boys and homosexual adults. But just as often they produce juvenile delinquents and adult criminals. In fact, there is every indication that male delinquency is directly related to sex identity; it occurs most frequently in boys with an insecure sex identity, boys who in their early years had no male model to imitate. In a very real sense, delinquency is an initiation rite which boys devise for themselves in order to prove and establish their masculinity when society provides no other means. Delinquency is the last ditch attempt to cut the apron strings.

Interestingly, one of the best methods of rehabilitating delinquent boys is to put them through a program of severe physical challenges and tests of endurance which are socially approved and rewarded. The rugged Outward Bound program has, for example, proven far more successful at reducing juvenile crime rates than the reform school system, where boys merely serve time and where they can demonstrate their masculinity only in acts of defiance. For delinquent boys the challenge of Outward Bound provides a double function: it is both a rite of passage and a proof of manhood. The rite of passage is not the only route to adult male status, however. Another way is to provide an earlier and more gradual initiation into the male world. In societies where boys are allowed to participate in the activities of men from the start there is no need for them to prove their manhood later in anti-social ways. In Chinese communities where this is the normal pattern, the phenomenon of delinquency is largely unknown.

Family Determinants of Sex Identity

What can parents do to foster a healthy sex identity in chidren? That question is a difficult one to answer since there is much disagreement today over what constitutes a healthy sex identity. It is possible, however, to show the consequences of certain family patterns. We know, for example, that certain types of father-son interaction generally result in the development of a strong masculine orientation in the boy. We are talking here, of course, about masculinity defined by traditional measures (assertiveness, aggressiveness, competence, initiative, independence), and not everyone subscribes to the desirability or usefulness of this traditional definition. Still, it is useful to know what kinds of fathers and mothers produce what kinds of sons and daughters.

Although most of the literature concerned with child raising is devoted to the mother's role, the bulk of the research indicates that the father plays the more crucial role in the development of sex identity. In most cases the father has a greater interest in sex differences than the mother; and he seems to exert more influence on the development of masculinity in his sons as well as femininity in his daughters. The first thing a father can do to promote a conventional sex identity in his children is to make himself available to them. Study after study shows that the absence of the father has deleterious effects on both sons and daughters. Father-absent girls are more likely than father-present girls to be overly dependent, to have difficulty in heterosexual adjustment, to have a low feminine self-concept, and to engage in delinquent behavior. Father-absent boys are likely to have less masculine interests, less conscience development, and more psychological problems than father-present boys.

Early father-absence is more likely to retard masculine development in boys and feminine development in girls than is late father-absence. This is in line with Money's thesis that there is a critical period for the learning of sex identity. E.M. Hetherington reported that boys who had become father-absent after the age of 4 were not appreciably different from father-present boys in regard to sex role measure. However, Biller and Baum in a study of junior high school boys found that boys who became father-absent before the age of 5 had significantly lower masculine self-concept, and masculine preference than did father-present boys. Moreover, another study by Biller showed that boys who became father-absent before the age of 4 had significantly less masculine sex role orientation than boys who became father-absent in their fifth year. The crucial period for learning sex identity, then, appears to take place before the age of 5. This does not mean, of course, that everything which happens to the child after the age of 5 is irrelevant to his sex identity. Nor does it mean that the degree of masculinity or femininity is irreversibly set before that age. Certain events or circumstances in adolescence or even in adulthood can help to compensate for earlier disorientations in sex identity.

The presence of the father is crucial for the development of sex identity and particularly crucial for the development of masculinity in boys. In an imperfect world, however, there will continue to be a great many homes in which the father is absent by reason of death, divorce, or desertion. In such situations it is best if the mother can find a surrogate father who will take an interest in the child. The role of masculine model could be assumed by a Big Brother, a scout leader, an uncle, a teacher, a male neighbor, or even an older adolescent. The child might also be encouraged to identify with a movie or television star, a sports hero, or a public figure. But, if the mother herself tries to play the role of masculine model, she may actually encourage femininity in her son since the boy will tend to identify with her sex rather than her behavior. The presence of an older brother, however, will often compensate somewhat for the father's absence. A number of studies have shown that father-absent boys with older brothers are less dependent and more masculine than father-absent boys without older brothers. Conversely, the presence of an older sister may only serve to reinforce the boy's feminine orientation.

The father who is available to his children is likely to be doing them a service. But availabiliy is not enough. Unless the father plays a masculine role within the family, the young boy will experience difficulty in making a strong masculine identification (by the same token, masculine acting fathers encourage femininity in their daughters). If the father plays a dominant, decision-making role it is likely that his son will develop a masculine self-concept as well as masculine interests. If the father is incapable of playing such a role or if the mother will not allow him to, the boy will likely find himself set on a course which leads away from masculine orientation and interests. In fact, father-present boys who perceive their fathers as ineffectual are more likely to suffer from sex role conflicts than boys who have no father. Outside the home the father may be decisive and competent but if he surrenders the masculine role within the family he will only succeed in providing a model to be avoided rather than emulated.

These patterns suggest that, despite the current rhetoric to the contrary, children do not flourish in families where household roles are interchangeable. Psychologist Urie Bronfenbrenner, in analyzing two studies, found that adolescents who came from families where fathers played a traditionally feminine role tended to be undependable. Those families in which sex roles are not differentiated, writes Bronfenbrenner, "produce young people who do not take initiative, look to others for direction and decision, and cannot be counted on to fulfill obligations." This was particularly true in families where the mother rather than the father dominated in setting limits for the child. In light of such findings one has to be suspect of the recent trend toward eliminating male and female role distinctions in the household. What little we do know of egalitarian families suggests that the rush to get rid of sex role polarities may be premature.

This does not mean that the father ought to be autocratic and iron-fisted; merely that he ought to be careful, if only for the sake of his son's masculinity, about relinquishing the traditional role of decision-maker and limit-setter. Playing such a role need not, of course, exclude the father from adopting certain aspects of the feminine role such as nurturance and affection. It does little good for the father to be dominant if he is not also warm and supportive. If he is merely a powerful and feared oppressor, it is unlikely that his children will be able to identify with him at all. Only when paternal dominance is combined with nurturance does it work in favor of the child's sex identity development; the over-controlling father interferes with the development of initiative and independence in his children. Interestingly, it often happens that a husband who is dominated by his wife will in turn dominate his son in a restrictive and controlling way. Unless the son is also allowed some areas of autonomy he is not likely to profit from his father's dominance.

What can the mother do if the father is absent or ineffectual? It is best under such circumstances is she can still encourage her children to maintain a positive image of the father or at least of the masculine role (it is equally desirable, of course, for the father to encourage a similar respect for the mother and for femininity). Unfortunately, this is usually difficult to do. If the father is absent due to abandonment or divorce, or if he is home but simply not living up to his responsibilities, the situation is ripe for the mother to criticize and devalue him. If the mother's derogatory view gets carried over to men in general, the children are likely to get caught in an uncomfortable bind: the son in order to please his mother may avoid the masculine role as long as possible, while the daughter may carry this negative view of males into her own relationships with men, thereby increasing the probability of their failure. Several studies indicate that this latter syndrome is particularly conspicuous in lower-class black families where the mother and other female relatives are dominant. The idea that "men are no good" becomes part of the daughter's inheritance, a self-fulfilling prophecy which perpetuates the matriarchal family. Biller's description of the problem is succinct: "Maternally based households seem to become like family heirlooms—passed from generation to generation."

By and large, the learning of sex role seems to be a matter of modeling. If sufficient nurturance is present, masculine fathers encourage masculinity in their sons, while feminine mothers encourage femininity in their daughters. Conversely, masculine mothers discourage femininity in their daughters, while feminine fathers discourage masculinity in their sons. The situation is somewhat different, however, between mother and son, and father and daughter. Thus, a masculine father encourages the development of femininity in his daughter, while a feminine mother encourages the development of masculinity in her son (when I use the word "encourage," I do not mean a positive conscious attempt to mold sex identity but an unconscious process resulting from the dynamic of the family structure). But if the parent does not play the appropriate role for his or her sex the child tends to model the sex rather than the behavior of the opposite sex parent. For example, the son of a masculine mother is prone to developing a feminine orientation. In summary, it seems safe to say that the best guarantee of an appropriate sex identity in the child is to be raised by a mother and father who feel comfortable with their respective sex role and sex identity.

Society's Role

While it is easy to list the factors which facilitate appropriate sex identities in children it is not so easy to supply them. It is rather pointless to remind a mother of the benefits of a father-present home when her husband has just deserted. It is fruitless to lecture a father on the importance of nurturance when he simply does not care about his children. It may require years of expensive psychotherapy before an affection-starved mother is able to release the stranglehold on her son. Obviously society has a responsibility to provide the conditions which make it possible for parents to carry out their roles and responsibilities. We are aware that various social, economic and demographic changes have combined to create a stripped-down family which seems increasingly incapable of sustaining its members. Yet these same forces have effectively eliminated the sense of community and mutual help which families could at one time fall back on when the going got rough.

It is beyond the scope of this essay to explore the avenues by which that sense of community might be restored, however I would like to suggest one method which directly relates to the formation of sex identity: the rite of passage. The problem of sex identity invariably reasserts itself during adolescence. No matter how neatly development may have progressed in childhood, the rapid changes of puberty often upset the balance so that a new resolution is required. Adolescence is, in effect, a second critical period for the establishment of sex identity.

Other societies, as I have mentioned previously, utilize this period to compensate for deficiencies or disorientations in the child's early sex identity development. Rites of passage are employed to solidify and reinforce feminine identity for the girl and masculine identity for the boy. In societies where the son is over-dependent on the mother, and where the fathers are uninvolved with family life, the initiation rite is considered particularly crucial for confirming the boy's transition from feminine to masculine identification. Yet in the United States where that family pattern is increasingly familiar, there are no rites of passage to speak of, and the rate of delinquency which is directly related to insecure sex identity continues to rise.

Obviously we have something to learn from these "primitive" cultures. It is high time that our society began to devise rites of passage which would be relevant to our culture but which could still serve to confirm and validate the sex identity of adolescents. The Outward Bound Program is one possible prototype. The C.C.C. of the Depression years might serve as another model. We might even look at the training programs of the Armed Forces for, despite its obvious drawbacks, the Army does often serve to transform the lives of young men. Our society is desperately in need of what William James called the "moral equivalent of war." He meant, as I have said elsewhere, "not an institution that would cater to men's violent instincts while avoiding actual bloodshed, but a cause or commitment that would summon the same energies, passions, and loyalties as does war. These energies are at their peak in adolescence, and it is a pity that when the young are looking for dragons to slay we hand them computer cards to fill out." Until society provides some avenues for adolescents to prove themselves in useful ways these energies will continue to be expended in pursuits which are often reckless and self-destructive.

Sex Identity and Personal Identity

In the preceding pages I have outlined the effect of certain family patterns on sex identity. I have, however, avoided using the words "healthy" or "unhealthy" to describe the resultant behavior; instead I have employed adjectives such as "appropriate," "traditional," or "conventional" to describe what has in the past been called "healthy" sex identity. Today we are not so sure that the older definitions of appropriate sex role behavior are valid. Indeed there is evidence to suggest that too much masculinity in the male or too much femininity in the female is a handicap.

Consider, for example, a longitudinal study conducted by psychologist Paul Mussen in which a group of highly masculine males were compared with a group of highly feminine males. During adolescence the highly masculine group possessed more qualities of self-confidence, self-acceptance, leadership, and dominance. By the time these men were in their 30's, however, the situation was reversed: the highly masculine group had shown a marked decline in measures of self-concept while the highly feminine group felt much better about themselves, and surpassed the other group in measures of confidence and self-acceptance. In another study aimed at measuring the social adjustment of girls, it was found that adolescent girls who exhibited unfeminine behavior were more popular among their peers than highly feminine girls. Another study of adolescent girls concluded that the best adjusted girls were similar to their unfeminine mothers, while the least well adjusted girls identified with their highly feminine mothers.

Extreme masculinity and extreme femininity appear to be decreasingly functional in our modern society where powerful machines do the work that once required strong men, and where fragility in women seems no longer desirable. Perhaps we are arriving at a stage of evolution where some parents would prefer their sons to be more feminine and their daughters more masculine. And perhaps in the near future, society will be more friendly to these children than it has in the past.

It is obvious then that until we decide what constitutes a healthy sex identity, no satisfactory answer can be given to parents who seek guidelines for fostering a healthy sex identity in their children. Our definition of healthy sex identity depends, in turn, on our definition of the healthy self; the discussion of sex identity cannot be divorced from the discussion of personal identity.

But, for this very reason, there always exists a danger that in our haste to find new and more comfortable sex identities and new and less restrictive sex roles we may latch on to definitions of health that are more faddish than functional. Currently we are witnessing a movement towards liberation from stereotypes, from roles, even liberation from the concept of sex identity. We should, according to the latest thinking be concerned with persons as persons, not as men and women. Unburdened of restrictive roles, men and women would be able to realize their full potential as human beings. This point of view has become so well entrenched among the educated classes, that one hesitates to subject it to criticism. Moreover, it has become associated with a number of obviously justified quests for political and social equality, and educational and economic opportunity. But interwoven with these laudable goals are some questionable assumptions about the nature of the healthy self. Anyone familiar with contemporary psychology will recognize that most of the vocabulary used to talk about role change is borrowed from a school of psychology known as the Human Potential Movement, or simply as "humanistic psychology". Human potentialists have been talking for decades about the need to actualize potentials, to develop the person rather than the role, to open up a wider range of options. Many of the assumptions which underlie the current thinking on sex roles are the same assumptions upon which humanistic psychology is founded.

These assumptions are worth looking at because they provide a model of the desirable—a picture of the healthy self. And this model—or better, interpretation—has been rather uncritically accepted as the proper one by a large number of people in our society. By and large when they talk about changing sex roles, they are talking about changing them in the direction of the Human Potential model.

According to this model of human nature, the healthy self (1) is fluid, (2) lives in the here-and-now, (3) is motivated primarily by a need for self-actualization. A closer look at this supposedly healthy model will show, however, that despite its desirable features it leaves very little room for qualities such as responsibility, commitment, cooperation, or love. A fluid self, a self which is always "in-process" or in a state of flux is not a responsible self; it can't be held accountable for yesterday's self or tomorrow's self. A self which exists primarily in the here-and-now will not be able to sustain commitments or maintain communities (or families, or love relationships). A person who is concerned mainly with his own self-actualization will tend to view commitments to others as a limitation on his freedom to grow; self-actualization easily slips over into self-absorption and selfishness.

Humanistic psychology is, in short, built upon assumptions which may in the long run prove to be dehumanizing. Until we know for sure what kind of persons we want, and until we know which aspects of sex identity are dispensable and which are not, we ought not be too hasty to liberate our children from their sexual identity. Although it may seem like a statement of the obvious, perhaps it is worth observing that sex identity gives us a sense of identity. It is one of the more important ways in which we define ourselves. When, for example, parents ask the doctor, "Is it a boy or a girl?" they are looking for a specific definition on which further definitions may be built—it is unlikely that any parent would be satisfied to hear, "It's a person." Children too seem adamant about defining themselves sexually. In fact, they seem more insistent than adults on maintaining the sexual polarities. Even children from the most liberated households will insist that "daddies don't cry". Little boys still seem intent on proving that they are little men; and little girls still play with miniature tea sets.

There is evidence that sex roles can be more flexible than they are at present, but sex identity seems to be a more crucial factor, and a less plastic one. As I have suggested before, one can't afford to be very experimental with sex roles unless one has a solid sense of sex identity. The currently fashionable flirtation with the notion of fluidity, with the philosophy of persons as persons, may be attractive to adults who already have a sense of who they are; they can afford themselves some redefinition. But to expect a child, who has not yet made any definitions, to be content with the nebulous identity of "person" is to mistake the nature of children. They are not cultivators of ambiguity. Rather, they are trying to make some sense of the complicated world they have so recently entered, and to do that they first need some sense of where they stand in it. Parents who have achieved flexible definitions of their own sexual status often find it difficult to understand why their children are so old-fashioned and literal minded about sex identity. They fail to realize that children too need some kind of identity--an identity which must of necessity be built on roles and definitions that are not overly complicated or ambigious. Most parents recognize the primitive wisdom by which an infant begins to differentiate himself from his mother in order to establish himslf as an independent being. Later on there will be time for him to rediscover his essential oneness with all other people. Perhaps the same wisdom is at work in the child who wants it to be made unmistakably clear that he belongs to this sex and not that one. Later on he will make his redefinitions.

REFERENCES

Biller, Henry B. *Father, Child, and Sex Role.* Lexington: D. C. Heath, 1971. Discusses the role of both fathers and mothers in fostering appropriate sex role behavior.

Green, Richard, M.D. *Sexual Identity Conflict in Children and Adults.* New York: Basic Books, 1974. Fascinating transcripts of interviews with transsexuals, feminine boys, masculine girls, and their relatives. Deals with causes and treatment in relatively non-technical language.

Kilpatrick, William. *Identity and Intimacy.* New York: Delacorte Press, 1975. A discussion of current trends in psychology and their effect on identity and intimacy.

Lynn, David B. *The Father: His Role in Child Development.* Monterey: Brooks/Cole Publishing Co., 1974. Summarizes a large body of research concerning father-child relationships; Lynn argues that the father plays the most important role in the development of the child's sex identity.

Money, John and Ehrhardt, Anke A. *Man and Woman, Boy and Girl.* New York: Mentor, 1974. A difficult but rewarding discussion of genes, hormones, and hermaphrodites based on extensive research by Money and his colleagues. The most comprehensive treatment of gender identity and sex errors yet published.

V.

THE MULTIPLE FUNCTIONS OF PLAY: A Review and Examination of the Piagetian and Psychoanalytic Points of View

By Ira Stamm

If we were each to ask ourselves, based on our experience as parents or even as former children, "Why children play?" the answers we would give might encompass a number of ideas about play. One of us might answer, "I played because it was fun." Another might reply, "I played at doing things that I later had to learn at school." Or an astute observer might comment, "When I was afraid of something like going to the doctor's office I would play a game of doctor. Somehow after playing at this game again and again I was no longer afraid of my next doctor's appointment." Not surprisingly, each of these comments about play forms the cornerstone of one or more theories of play. These comments reflect the separate notions that children play because (1) it is fun, (2) through play the child learns about himself and the world in which he participates, and (3) play enables the child to assimilate overpowering emotional feelings and experiences. Surprisingly, most theories of play view play as fulfilling only one of these functions to the exclusion of the others. This runs counter to our point of view that play may fulfill multiple functions. In one moment the child may play because play *is* fun, in another moment he may play a game to learn something new about his world, and in yet another moment he may play to become more comfortable with a potentially frightening situation.

But why should parents, educators or psychologists concern themselves about children's play? Why bring the conceptual lens of the academic classroom to focus on something as unobtrusive and innocuous as children's play? The fact that children spend a large part of their childhood at play does not appear to be a casual occurrence. While play is often an effortless and natural activity, a closer look at play reveals that the fun of play is accompanied by the child's wish and capacity to learn and to experience more about himself, others, and his world and to adapt to internal and external changes. Play is simply the medium through which these processes occur.

This essay will examine the multiple functions of play through a review of Jean Piaget's play theory and the psychoanalytic theory of play. These theories provide the conceptual frameworks that offer the most meaningful understanding of the play process. They also share a common developmental framework and in some ways offer complementary explanations of not only play but other psychological processes as well. The review of these theories will be followed by a critical examination of them. Suggestions as to how some of the ideas inherent in these theories might be brought together into an updated version of the psychoanalytic theory of play are offered in the conclusion.

Jean Piaget's Theory of Play

Piaget's theory of play is presented in his book *Play, Dreams, and Imitation in Childhood* in which he links play closely to his theory of intellectual development. Jean Piaget is a developmental psychologist, born in 1896 in Switzerland, who for more than half a century has studied the ways in which children gain knowledge about their world. Many of his writings are based on the detailed observation he made of the intellectual growth of his two children. Piaget's systematic observation of his children as they talked, played, and otherwise interacted with their world was linked to this asking children questions about how they perceived and understood their world. Piaget, then, using this "clinical method" of asking questions tried to understand children through what children could tell him about their experiences. Piaget recognized that the child's view of the world did not consist of a carefully copied or mirrored reflection of the way the world appears to adults. Rather, each child creates a view of the world based on his ability to appreciate reality.'

An example may illustrate how the child's perception of the world differs from an adult's. An adult looking at a checker board and checkers makes certain almost automatic observations. He knows that in front of him is a game of checkers, that there are twelve red checkers and twelve black checkers, and he knows how to play the game. The infant looking at the same checker board and checkers would hardly notice any of the distinguishing characteristics of the checkers or checker board, let alone understand their purpose. He might not even be aware of the difference between the red and black checkers. His interaction with the checkers might be simply to pick up the checkers and place them in his mouth, since his reality at this very early level of development is determined by his very modest capacity to touch or grasp objects and place them in his mouth.

As this infant matured his capacity to appreciate the nature of the checkers would undergo some changes. He might first begin to notice that the red and black checkers did not look alike, but he would not think in terms of "black" and "red" since he would not have a concept of colors. Eventually, as he progressed further in his intellectual understanding of the world, he would come to an appreciation of colors. First he would simply call a red checker "red" in an imitative way after hearing his mother refer to that specific object as red. Later he would understand that the word "red" is used to designate objects that look alike because they have the same color. Focusing on the number of checkers, the infant or young child would have little regard for the number of checkers. They would appear to be simply a mass of wooden or plastic objects. Soon he might be able to count "one, two, three checkers" again in an imitative fashion because he hears others counting, but again he would have no real understanding of the concept of number. As he grew up and learned more about his world he would learn to count to twelve and understand that counting is a way of ordering and comprehending a number of items. Finally, only at a later stage of development would the child appreciate the function of the checkers, that is, a game with rules, and played by two people.

The example of the checkers illustrates several things. First, it illustrates how the child constructs his own theory of knowledge or view of the world based on his intellectual capacity at a given point in time. Second, the child's capacity to understand his world goes through developmental transformations so that the infant's perception of the world becomes the child's perception of the world which in turn develops into the adult's perception of the world. Third, the level of the child's play will be closely linked to his intellectual level of development. As the example demonstrates, the infant's play with the checker set will be very different from the child's, adolescent's, or adult's. The infant will put the pieces to his mouth, the child may use the checkers as building blocks or create his own rules for a unique game of checkers, and the adolescent or adult finally might use the checker set as it was intended to be used.

Organization and Adaptation

In his theory of intellectual development, Piaget proposes two fundamental characteristics of intelligence and cognitive functioning which are inherent properties of the human mind. The first characteristic is organization. This implies that all intelligent mental functioning follows the general organizational principles of mind. Implicit in this concept is the presence of psychological structures or schemata capable of becoming organized into intelligent activity. A schema is any such organized piece of intelligent activity, either behavioral or mental. The infant grasping a checker and bringing it to his mouth is exercising a "grasping" schema, and the child counting twelve checkers is exercising a schema involving numerical concepts.

The second basic characteristic of intelligent mental activity is adaptation. All thought and behavior that is intelligent is essentially adaptive and Piaget roughly defines intelligence as adaptive behavior. Adaptive behavior allows the infant or child to come to terms with its environment.

To explain intellectual development Piaget proposes that the process of adaptation occurs through the mutually reciprocal processes of assimilation and accomodation. Assimilation occurs when the organism takes new material into its already existing psychic structure. But quite often a new piece of information cannot be assimilated by the already existing psychic structure. The organism then faces the alternative of either rejecting this new material or of modifying its own psychic structure to accommodate the novel material. Accommodation is the process wherein the modification of a present psychological structure or schema occurs.

Assimilation and accommodation are complementary processes and are to be viewed as two sides of adaptation. Every act of assimilation involves an act of accommodation and vice versa. The constant process of assimilation and accommodation often leave the organism in a state of disequilibrium. It is in this state of disequilibrium that the organism learns and develops. A state of equilibrium occurs when assimilation and accomodation have reached a plateau and there is no further material to assimilate or no further accommodation to be made.

Piaget has described several kinds of assimilation. Functional assimilation is the form of assimilation that has the greatest relevance for play. As the infant begins to make sucking motions or to exercise its limbs or fingers, it is making use of functional assimilation. It is acquiring a new skill. Through the repeated exercise of these movements it is mastering these movements, and in so far as the infant is capable of knowing, is developing an intelligent sensori-motor understanding of this skill.

The Appearance of Play

But eventually the infant reaches a point wherein additional exercise or repetition does nothing to further the development of this adaptive form of behavior. The infant seems to engage in these excessive manipulations for the pure pleasure it brings to him. At this point he makes use of assimilation in its purest form without regard to intelligent or adaptive purposes. This use of functional assimilation is what Piaget defines as play. As Piaget states, "Play...proceeds by relaxation of the effort at adaptation and by maintenance or exercise of activities for the mere pleasure of mastering them and acquiring thereby a feeling of virtuosity of power."

In a later passage Piaget elaborates upon this view:

Play begins, then, with the first dissociation between assimilation and accommodation. After learning to grasp, swing, throw, etc. which involve both an effort of accommodation to new situations, and an effort of repetition, reproduction, and generalization, the child sooner or later (often even during the learning period) grasps for the pleasure of grasping, swings for the sake of swinging, etc. In a word, he repeats his behavior not in any further effort to learn or to investigate, but for the mere joy of mastering it and of showing off to himself his own power of subduing reality. Assimilation is dissociated by subordinating it and tending to function by itself, and from then on practice play occurs.

For Piaget, intellectual or cognitive growth occurs as the child acquires or develops more advanced schemata for participating in his world. Advancement along the developmental ladder occurs through the unfolding of new and more advanced psychological schemata in the child as he interacts with his world. In other words, Piaget proposes that the child's cognitive processes go through a developmental process. This development is analogous to the child's physical growth. Just as a child crawls until he is physically able to walk, and walks until he is physically able to run, his thinking functions in cognitively primitive ways until his mental processes mature to the point where he can think in more mature ways.

During the child's infancy through the second year of life, the child's intellectual functioning is linked to his sensori-motor involvement with the world. Piaget lists six sub-stages of play within these first two years that correspond to the six sub-stages of the sensori-motor stage of growth.

In the first sub-stage of intellectual growth and play the infant's earliest intelligent and adaptive behaviors are the exercise of his reflexes, primarily the sucking reflex. When the infant continues his sucking movement after his hunger is satisfied he is playing. However, Piaget thinks that even much of this sucking serves an adaptive purpose as these sucking movements develop the infant's proficiency at sucking. With further proficiency, though, play becomes increasingly differentiated from adaptive behavior. In the second sub-stage of cognitive development, the infant begins to make random movements, some of which lead to gratification. He repeats this event and thereby develops a well organized schema. He may look at objects for long periods of time or continually grasp at objects. When these actions no longer serve the development of a cognitive schema and when they become play is not often clear.

In a third sub-stage of intellectual growth the infant derives pleasure from causing things to happen to objects. He learns that he is able to bring about some activity. For example, he learns that if he lifts and shakes a rattle it will produce a sound. His initial attempts at such an activity help him understand what he can and cannot cause to happen. In this sense the activity involves adaptation. However, at some point the infant knows quite well that if he shakes the rattle he will produce a sound and his continued efforts at shaking the rattle now become play. He makes the sound because it is fun.

In sub-stage four the child begins to apply already acquired schemata to new situations. For example, the child in sub-stage three may have learned the schema of reaching for and removing an object. Now in sub-stage four he may employ this schema to remove a toy from behind a barrier. Soon, however, he may repeatedly remove the barrier for the sake of removing the barrier forgetting about the toy altogether. When the child now repeats this action, laughing as he does, he then is playing. In the fifth sub-stage it is often the novel relationship among schema that excites the child and accounts for his play. Schemata are combined together in sub-stage four, too, but typically they are well known schemata combined in a new way. In sub-stage five the schemata themselves have a new quality to them and the play based on them has more the quality of play. For example, Piaget cites the child who puts a pin down with one hand away from himself and then picks it up with the other hand, repeating this eventually in a playful way. The schema of putting an item down with one hand and picking it up with another is new and inventive, although the actions of picking up and putting down an object are well exercised schema.

In the sixth sub-stage, the beginning of thought, the child finally becomes capable of symbolic play. Piaget cites his observations of J. who saw a cloth that reminded her of her pillow. She grabbed the cloth, put an edge of it in her hand, sucked her thumb and lay down as though going to sleep. In this example, J. has added the element of "make believe" to the ritualized play of going to sleep that she had exercised earlier in her development. However, two new elements are added now to the exercise of previous schemata. First, the child no longer exercises the schema with the familiar object, (the pillow). Instead, she applies the schema to new objects that do not necessarily serve the functions of intelligence and adaptation, that is, the child does not ordinarily sleep with her head on a piece of cloth. Second, the inclusion of these different objects in the schema does not expand the schema in any meaningful or intelligent way but only serves the purpose of allowing the child to exercise the schema in a pleasurable or playful way. As Piaget maintains, "It is the union of these two conditions—application of the schema to inadequate objects and evocation for pleasure—which in our opinion characterizes the beginning of pretence."

The Development of Games

After examining the development of play in the first two years of life, Piaget shifts to classifying the games a child plays at each developmental phase in his life. There are hree stages of games: *practice games, symbolic games,* and *games with rules.* Each corresponds roughly to the three major stages of intellectual development: sensori-motor level (0-2 years), the pre-operational or representational level (2-7 years), and the operational level (7-11 years). The infant's games through the first 18 months of life are practice games, the result of functional assimilation and playful repetition. Each time a new behavior or skill is acquired by the child he seeks to assimilate it. Once the new skill is assimilated into an already existing schema, the child often continues to play at the schema.

Practice games are followed by symbolic games at about 18 months of life. In practice games the content matters little since what the child plays at or what he says verbally is done only for the point of exercise. In the symbolic games what the child imagines or says becomes very important to him since he is trying to communicate something through the symbolic transformation he is verbalizing or acting upon. The most basic symbolic structure is that of the *symbolic schema.* The symbolic schema is of special interest and importance because it marks the transition between sensori-motor and symbolic thought. By definition, the *symbolic schema* is "the reproduction of sensory motor schema outside its context and in the absence of it usual objective."

Three statements may be made about the symbolic schema as it is used in play. First, there is no adaptive purpose or intent when it occurs in play. Second, symbolism is used. Third, this symbolism is related to the child's specific and concrete behaviors. The child pretends at sleeping, eating, washing, but he is the one who performs these actions. At a later point in his development he can pretend that someone other than himself is sleeping, eating, or washing.

Piaget presents a detailed analysis of the mental structures operative during different stages of the child's symbolic period. This period occurs roughly from 18 months to 7 years. Only a few of these specific structures and forms of play need concern us here and the reader is referred to Piaget's book on play for a detailed analysis. Piaget notes that symbolic play often allows the child an opportunity to reproduce or extend his real world. The characters created at this stage are usually sympathetic to the child's point of view or serve as a mirror of his world. Later on, Piaget notes, instead of trying to reproduce reality in his play for the pleasure it brings the child tries to alter it. For example, Piaget notes that J. once was forbidden to play with water because it was being used for other purposes. To compensate for this J. took her cup, went over to the wash basin and pretended to pour water with her cup.

Sometimes this compensatory play allows the child to work through upsetting feelings. For example, Piaget mentions that L., age 2 years, 9 months, was afraid of a tractor that stood in a field near the house. One day L. commented as she held her doll that "dolly told me she would like to ride on a machine like that." At a later age L. was afraid to play with friends who were organizing a game of theater at a nearby barn. She therefore created her own game of theater with her dolls. In yet another kind of play the child does not compensate for an uncomfortable aspect of reality, but instead tries to assimilate a reality that has been difficult for him. In this play the child symbolically dissociates his play from the once painful context of reality. This allows him to assimilate that reality through his play.

Games with rules may start during the symbolic phase but their main occurrence is in the third phase between 7 and 11. Games with rules appear mainly at this later age because they are closely linked to the child's growing socialization. Piaget calls games with rules "the lucid activity of the socialized being." In the evolution of play, symbolic play replaced practice play when thought appeared, and now games with rules replace symbolic play when the child enters certain social relationships. This socialization is a prerequisite for games with rules because other people are the source of the rules.

Piaget differentiates between two kinds of rules as they occur in games at this age. There are rules which are transmitted from other children or adults and there are rules that emerge spontaneously as the children engage in social play. The rules transmitted from others constitute "institutional" rules that may be handed down from generation to generation. Spontaneous rules, however, are of more direct relevance to a theory of play. They emerge when practice play and symbolic play become increasingly socialized.

The brief look we have taken at Piaget's theory of play covers only the highlights. The theory is developed in greater detail by Piaget in *Play, Dreams, and Imitations in Childhood* (1951). His theory of play offers a coherent and well thought out exposition of the play of children. Essentially, though, Piaget separates play from intelligent and adaptive thought. He belongs to that theoretical school of thought that maintains children play because it is fun. While he allows that play may serve other functions, his emphasis is on the enjoyment or fun of play. Our thesis is that play may fulfill multiple functions. In order to examine other possible functions of play, another prominent viewpoint, the psychoanalytic theory of play, will be discussed.

The Psychoanalytic Theory of Play:
Robert Waelder and Sigmund Freud

The classic psychoanalytic statement about play is contained in a paper by Robert Waelder, "The Psychoanalytic Theory of Play," which includes consideration of Sigmund Freud's original contribution to the theory of play. Waelder (1900-1967), a psychoanalyst trained in Vienna, was known as both a prolific psychoanalytic writer and an outstanding teacher of psychoanalysis. Waelder notes first, in his article on play, that a child's play appears to be rooted in experience. The child seems to play at activities with which he is familiar, through an involvement with the activities as either a participant or as a witness. The child may play at being a parent, relative, or workman and he may act in any of the ways he perceives these people as acting.

The child appears to act out pleasurable aspects of his experience, or to obtain through his play pleasure similar to that which he obtained in his experiences. It would appear, therefore, that the child's play is in the service of the pleasure principle. For example, the child who plays at being a nurse or teacher expresses her wish to be grown up and to be a nurse or teacher herself. This is a motif common to many children's game. If the child enacts an automobile ride, she may be recreating an earlier pleasurable scene. Much of the child's play seems to be an attempt to recapture the pleasure of earlier events and scenes.

But some of the child's play seems in direct contradiction to the pleasure principle. The child who goes to the dentist and then spends the rest of the afternoon at home with his friends playing a game of dentist surely is not trying to regain the pleasurable aspects of his visit to the dentist. The trip to the dentist must have been painful for him, a trip he would choose to forget as quickly as possible. The pleasure principle does not provide an understanding of the child's re-enactment of this painful event. How, then, is this phenomenon to be understood?

Waelder notes a systematic course of the child's play. On the day of his visit to the dentist the child will play at the event repeatedly with great intensity. The next day he may play at the game several times but with less intensity. Eventually, the frequency and intensity of his play diminish. This suggests a major thesis about play, namely, that the child's play gradually allows the child to assimilate experiences that have been unpleasant.

The Repetition Compulsion in Play

As the child attempts to assimilate overwhelming experiences, the psychoanalytic concept of the "repetition compulsion" becomes important to an understanding of children's play. At any time a person may have an experience which is too difficult for him to assimilate psychologically. The experience lingers in the mind. Because the process of assimilation is incomplete the unassimilated component of the experience seeks some form of re-expression. This takes the form of a compulsion with a need to discharge itself. However, there is also a need to assimilate the powerful experience through repetition with diminished intensity. Thus, through the repetition compulsion the person, in a passive way, attempts to replicate the experience to which he has been subjected and, in an active way, attempts to master through assimilation the experience to which he has been exposed. As Freud described it:

> The ego, which has passively experienced the trauma, now actively repeats an enfeebled reproduction of it, hoping that in the course of this, it will be able through its own action to direct it. We know that the child takes the same attitude to all impressions painful to him, reproducing them in the form of a game; through this manner of proceeding from passivity to activity he seeks to master mentally the impressions received from life (*Hemmung, Symptom und Angst;* in Waelder, 1933, pp.214-215).

Freud also expressed a similar idea in two additional passages which deal more directly with play.

> We see the children repeat in their play everything that has made a great impression on them in actual life, that they thereby abreact the strength of the impression, and so to speak make themselves masters of the situation (*Beyond the Pleasure Principle,* 1920; in Waelder, 1933, p. 215).
> In the play of children we seem to arrive at the conclusion that the child repeats even the unpleasant experiences because through his own activity he gains a far more thorough mastery of the strong impression than was possible by mere passive experience. Every fresh repetition seems to strengthen this mastery for which the child strives...(*Beyond the Pleasure Principle,* 1920; in Waelder, 1933, p.215).

Waelder (1933) notes that the concept of the repetition compulsion makes an important assumption about the nature of the person in relation to the outer world. A person can assimilate experience only in manageable parcels and cannot take in any and all stimuli that comes his way. When a person is confronted with a potential psychological overload, he is assisted by the repetition compulsion which allows him to assimilate sensory experience in more manageable units. The repetition compulsion is not a blind driving urge seeking pure repetition. Rather, it is the activity through which unfinished processes attain completion and through which maximum assimilation is achieved.

Waelder maintains that the processes involved in a child's play are often similar to those of the repetition compulsion. The child who goes to the dentist is confronted with what for him is a powerful and overwhelming experience. The play that ensues is his attempt to master that experience through the mechanism of the repetition compulsion. He is very much like the adult who attempts to assimilate a traumatic or equally overwhelming situation. As the child gets older, and his capacity to assimilate troubling experiences increases, he has less need to do so through play.

A major psychoanalytic thesis about play is summarized in Waelder's statement, "According to the conclusions arrived at by psychoanalysis, play may be a process like a repetition compulsion, by which excessive experiences are divided into small quantities, reattempted and assimilated in play."

Other Characteristics of Processes in Play

Assimilation of "excessive experiences" is one of the defining characteristics of play. What are some of the other characteristics of play? Another characteristic of play is that it occurs at a point in time when there is physical and mental growth. Waelder thinks it is not merely coincidental that play occurs at a time when the child's mind is developing and hence most malleable. Play allows the child to accommodate himself to a wide range of experiences. If assimilation through play were not available, many experiences would act upon the child with such force as to impede his functioning and curtail his growth. With the resource of play the child may encounter novel situations and stimuli with bravado and develop broader and deeper adaptive capacities. As the child matures, he has other processes available to him through which he may assimilate overpowering experiences. At that point play no longer maintains its critical life-sustaining and growth facilitating function.

Another distinctive characteristic of play is the tendency for fantasy and reality to overlap. This is essential if the play is to enable the child to ingest manageable pieces of reality. The inability to deal with initial reality leads to the fantasy embellishment of reality in the child's play. Through his fantasy play the child masters reality. At times the play of a child represents a departure from reality, as when a child pretends he can fly or when he pretends that animals can talk like humans. Or the departure may be from taboos and prohibitions, as when in his play he acts out hitting his parent or younger sibling. Waelder notes that play is similar in several ways to both fantasy and daydreams. Play, fantasies, and daydreams share two common functions. Each seeks instinctual gratification and each represents an attempt to assimilate disagreeable experiences.

Most fantasies represent unfulfilled wishes. In less common fantasies a painful event may occur over and over again in the mind of the person. In this instance the fantasy activity plays the same role as in play, the repetitive nature of the fantasy is the person's attempt to assimilate the alien event.

How, then, are play and fantasy different? Freud in "The Relation of the Poet to Day-Dreaming," discusses this difference:

> Every playing child behaves like a poet, in that he creates a world of his own, or more accurately expressed, he transposes things into his own world according to a new arrangement which is to his liking. It would be unfair to believe that he does not take this world seriously; on the contrary, he takes his play very seriously, he spends large amounts of affect on it. The antithesis of play is reality, not seriousness. The child differentiates his play world from reality very well in spite of all the affective cathexis, and gladly lets his imaginary objects and relationships depend upon the tangible and visible things in the real world. Only this dependence differentiates the "play" of children from "fantasying."

Waelder's interpretation of this statement is that play is merely the embellishment of real objects with fantasy. Both the child and the adult can differentiate the real world from the play world. In the normal adult mind this distinction is always clear-cut. But the child's mind allows a greater ease in embellishing real objects with fantasy. When the child does so he is playing.

At the end of his article on play Waelder suggests that the psychoanalytic contribution to the theory of play can be summarized with the following phrases:

> Instinct Of Mastery; Wish Fulfillment; Assimilation Of Overpowering Experiences According To The Mechanism Of The Repetition Compulsion; Transformation From Passivity To Activity; Leave Of Absence From Reality And From The Superego; Fantasies About Real Objects.

Waelder's article on the psychoanalytic theory of play has been examined in some detail because it still remains one of the most important psychoanalytic documents on this subject. It reviews, in part, Freud's contributions to the theory of play and also examines the relationship between play and other psychological phenomena such as neuroses, day dreams and creative imagination.

Erikson's Analysis of Play

Since the publication of Waelder's now classic article on play in 1933, many psychoanalytic thinkers have written about play, updating the psychoanalytic theory of play and keeping it abreast with the latest developments in psychoanalytic theory. Prominent among these has been a contemporary psychoanalyst, Erik Erikson, who has contributed greatly to the present day psychoanalytic understanding of man, but who has also been able through his lucid writings to translate the complexities of psychoanalytic theory into terms that most students and lay people can understand. While the focus of the classical psychoanalytic proposition of play is on the role of play in mastering overpowering experiences, the writings of Erikson and more recent psychoanalytic thinkers has been on the role of play in enabling the child to learn about and participate in his world. One frame of reference used by Erikson and other writers is the developmental one.

Erikson notes that in the first stage of play the infant centers his attention about his own body. This level of play he labels "autocosmic play". It is autocosmic because shortly after the child has exercised the parts of his body and familiarized himself with them he begins to use the parts of his body in a limited way to explore the immediate world around him. However, his exploratory interest is not in the service of learning more about the outer world per se, but instead enables the child to learn more about his own body. Erikson cites as examples the infant crying out to the mother in different tones to see what response each tone will bring; or he may explore the mother's body with his hands to learn more about his body in relation to hers. Erikson views such autocosmic play as the child's first orientation to the geography of the world and his first play sessions as his first geography lessons.

The next phase of play Erikson labels the "microsphere." The microsphere represents the child's small world of his own manageable toys. Erikson invokes the metaphor of the microsphere as the harbor to which the child may return when his ego needs an overhaul. The microsphere is a critical point in the child's development. If he learns to use toys constructively to master anxieties and to develop skills then he can continue on to the next stage of psychological growth. But if he uses toys in an infantile way such as by destroying them, or does not use them to master life's encounters, then he is apt to regress in his functioning to even more immature modes of psychological functioning.

The third and final stage of play occurs when the child reaches nursery school age and enters the "macrosphere." This is a social world in which the child shares his play with others. However, within Erikson's psychoanalytic model each developmental phase becomes integrated into and subordinated to the developmental phase above it. Thus the child whose main play may be in the macrosphere, still retains the capacity to use microsphere and autocosmic play at times. In fact, one major task of the macrosphere stage is learning when to engage in social play and when to play alone. In times of stress the child will have to make use of solitary play to master his anxiety, and at such moments play in the microsphere is preferred.

Erikson differentiates between the play of the child and adult. When the adult plays he moves sideways into a different reality whereas the child in play is stepping not sideways but forward to new phases of growth. Erikson offers a major proposition about child's play, "I propose the theory that the child's play is the infantile form of the human ability to deal with experience by creating model situations and to master reality by experiment and planning." In another passage from the chapter "Toys and Reasons" in *Childhood and Society* (1950) Erikson comments:

> Play, then is an attempt to synchronize the bodily and the social processes with

the self...Yet the emphasis, I think, should be on the ego's need to master the various
areas of life and especially those in which the individual finds his self, his body, and his
social role wanting and trailing.

Erikson, like Waelder and S. Freud, notes that the child's play may have
a "unique meaning." This is the personal meaning that motivates the
child to play at a particular activity or to play out a symbolic theme. Is
the child interested in exploring new and distant places as he acquires
new skills and greater mobility in order to put these new acquisitions to a
test? Or is he interested in remote places because he is angry at his
parents and wants to leave them far behind? The unique meaning of a
child's play can only be ascertained by careful observation of its form
and content and of the verbal expressions and feelings that are associated
with it.

In making an assessment of the meaning of the child's play, many
factors must be taken into consideration including the level of the child's
emotional development. Erikson cites the frequent concern of mothers
who think their sons must be in a "destructive stage" because they will
build a tower of blocks and then take delight in knocking it down. Rather
than take this as evidence that the child is in a destructive stage, Erikson
assumes that this play is related to the child's recent experience of learning to walk, when he first stood up and then, like the tower, collapsed.
The child is doing to the tower what he himself experienced as a toddler.
This allows the child to turn a passive experience of having fallen down
into an active experience, causing the tower to collapse. It also
strengthens his feeling of adequacy as a young boy to know there is
something weaker than him. He also knows that the tower will not
avenge his punitive action as might his siblings or parents.

Play Configurations of Boys and Girls

One of Erikson's major contributions to the psychoanalytic
understanding of play has been his research and written commentary
about the play configurations of boys and girls. In *Childhood and
Society,* Erikson reports on the results of a study he conducted with ten,
eleven, and twelve year old boys and girls at the University of California.

Erikson invited each subject into a room that contained a table with
a random selection of toys on it. He then instructed the boys or girls to
create an imaginary scene with the toys as though they were making a
movie. Much data was accumulated from this study but what Erikson
found most striking was the difference in the play configurations of boys
and girls. Boys tended to build structures, buildings and towers, whereas
girls built enclosed or hollow structures such as the interior of a house.
However, boys also made structures that conveyed the towers had fallen
down and girls also made structures that were open. Boys might build

ruins (fallen structures) and girls semi-enclosed houses. This suggested to Erikson that boys' play configurations were placed along a "high-low" dimension whereas play configurations of girls were along an "open-closed" dimension.

Although a child's experience is rooted in a biological template, Erikson comments that the child's play configurations will be modified by his culture and his inner psychodynamic makeup. Erikson concludes that in child's play there is the interpenetration of the biological, cultural and psychological.

Other Psychoanalytic Views

While other psychoanalytic writings about play deserve inclusion in any discussion about play, we will only be able to comment on those ideas that expand upon or differ from the ideas about play already discussed. L. Peller agrees with the basic psychoanalytic propositions about play, but adds that play can be viewed as "regression in the service of the ego", a concept first introduced into psychoanalytic theory to explain creativity. Both the artist, poet, writer, and the child at play voluntarily suspend part of their control over unconscious feelings and processes to allow the emergence of preconscious or unconscious fantasies in their play or artistic creations.

Peller, Anna Freud and D. W. Winnicott present developmental analyses of play similar to that of Erikson, noting that the child's play progresses from play with his body, to play with objects and people in his world. A. Freud and Winnicott note that at some point in his or her development, the child makes use of a "transitional object" such as a favorite blanket or stuffed animal. The child becomes extremely attached to this object and becomes quite distraught if it is altered or lost. This "transitional object" enables the child to make a gradual transition from his earliest preoccupation with his body and himself to an increasing awareness and investment in others and the world about him. The child plays with transitional objects that possess the characteristics for him of both his inner subjective experience and of external reality but that are like neither.

F. Alexander takes exception to the traditional psychoanalytic view of play, resurrecting a "surplus energy" view of play that contains some ideas similar to Piaget's perspective of play. Alexander believes that most organisms expend their energy in the service of adaptation and survival. But as the organism makes more efficient use of its energies, it develops a surplus reservoir of energy. This energy is then expended in play, and is expended simply because play is fun.

P. Greenacre suggests that the repetition of upsetting events through play also serves to develop the child's sense of reality. The child at play assimilates new experiences and incorporates them into his view of reality. Everyone is familiar with the experience of looking again for the second time because they "couldn't believe their eyes". This second look enables us to assimilate an aspect of reality that was too difficult to assimilate at first glance. Children's play may also serve a similar purpose.

The concept "instinct of mastery" as used by Waelder denotes the mastery of overpowering experiences through the child's assimilation of them. Greenacre reminds us of the different psychoanalytic meaning of the "instinct to master" to describe the infant or child's acquisition of new skills and his mastery of those skills. Perhaps, then, play allows the child to learn more about his world and to master those skills he uses in learning about the world.

The Multiple Functions of Play

Our purpose in reviewing the different theories and ideas about play has been to demonstrate that play fulfills a broad spectrum of functions. The conceptualizations of play advocated by the theorists reviewed in this essay fall along three lines of thoughts. (1) Piaget, along with Alexander, believes that children play simply because it is fun. Play fulfills no adaptive or intelligent purpose but occurs only because children enjoy doing it. (2) S. Freud and Waelder propose that the central function of play is to help children master anxiety and assimilate overpowering experiences. (3) Erikson and others acknowledge the defensive functions of play but add that play develops the child's sense of reality and expands his knowledge of his world. However, each theorist discussed does not adhere strictly to one view of play. Although Piaget maintains that play is non-adaptive, he speaks like a psychoanalyst when he discusses the compensatory or cathartic functions of play. And Waelder sounds like Piaget or Alexander when he acknowledges (as he does elsewhere in his article) that the playful reaching of infants occurs because the child finds this pleasurable.

There emerges from the concepts of play reviewed in this essay a unified psychoanalytic view of play that touches upon many of these ideas. Simply stated, play fulfills multiple functions. To enumerate those major functions it may be said that:

(1)   Play is a medium that expands a child's awareness of reality and enables him to assimilate knowledge about his world; it also enables him to master those skills he needs to learn about and to know his world.

(2)   Play serves a defensive function in enabling the child to assimilate overpowering emotional feelings or experiences and to master anxiety.

(3)   Play may occur simply because it is fun, out of the need of the child to experience pleasure or to have a good time. Conceptually, play occurs as "regression in the service of the ego."

The point of view that play serves no adaptive purpose must be rejected. Each function of play, whether it enables the child to learn about the world, to master anxiety, or to have a good time is subservient to the efforts at adaptation and survival made by all living organisms. The child's play at any given point in time may encompass one or several of the functions of play. Some play clearly may be just fun, or anxiety reducing, or educational. At other times it may be more difficult to distinguish which function of play is in operation.

Conclusion

What are the implications for us as students, educators, or parents of understanding the way in which play serves different purposes for the child? The reader should develop from this essay an appreciation of the importance of understanding the *meaning* of human behavior. Both Piaget and the psychoanalyst have systematically sought to understand the meaning of children's play, whether through Piaget's "clinical method," the psychoanalyst's "play interview" or by controlled empirical research. From such systematic inquiry into the meaning and purpose of play emerged the understanding of play presented in this essay. From that understanding of play evolves the psychoanalyst's use of play as a modality for the treatment of emotionally ill children. But for those of us who work or live with children in different capacities, as teachers or parents, the significance of play should now be more apparent. Play is an indispensable aspect of childhood. Through play the child can learn things about himself, about others, and about his environment. He can weather his emotional ups and downs, and he can enjoy the fun and relaxation all children need. Play can be an important barometer of the past, present and future. The child playing out some unpleasant fantasy may be telling us something about an unhealed emotional wound or about his apprehension of the future. Dull, monotonous play says something about how the child feels emotionally or how he functions intellectually. Intelligent, creative play tells you the child is alert, bright, and happy. If one cannot understand what a child is feeling or experiencing through his words, then perhaps one can understand more about the child through his play.

It may be redundant to conclude an essay on play with a recommendation that educators and parents create an education or home atmosphere conducive to children's play. Yet there are some people who may feel that play is the folly of youth, a folly that distracts children the more important tasks of scholarship and hard work. However, the understanding of play developed in this paper suggests that play can co-exist with learning and other tasks of childhood and in many instances facilitate the accomplishment of those tasks.

REFERENCES

Alexander, F. "A Contribution to the Theory of Play." *Psychoanalytic Quarterly*, 1958, 27, pp.175-193. Important only in that it varies from the traditional psychoanalytic point of view in suggesting that play occurs because it is fun.

Erikson, E.H. *Childhood and Society*. New York: W.W. Norton and Co., 1950. A basic readable book about children and psychoanalytic theory. One of those important books that should be read by any student interested in children even if he is not interested in psychoanalytic theory.

Freud, A. *Normality and Pathology in Childhood*. New York: International Universities Press, 1965. An excellent though highly technical psychoanalytic writing about, as its title states, normal and pathological development in childhood.

Freud, S. (1908) "The Relation of the Poet to Daydreaming." *On Creativity and the Un-conscious: Papers on the Psychology of Art, Literature, Love Religion*. New York: Harper & Row, 1958. Through a discussion of poetry, creativity, and day-dreaming, Freud touches on the subject of children's play. An interesting paper.

Ginsburg, H. and Opper, S. *Piaget's Theory of Intellectual Development*. New York: Prentice-Hall, Inc., 1969. One of the best overall books about Piaget's theory of cognitive development. Written clearly enough to provide an excellent introduction to Piaget, yet scholarly enough to be useful to the more advanced student of Piaget.

Greenacre, P. "Play in Relation to Creative Imagination." *Psychoanalytic Study of the Child*. New York: International Universities Press, 1959, Vol. XIV, pp. 61-80. An excellent article on play by an eminent psychoanalytic writer. An important writing for understanding the evolution of the psychoanalytic view of play.

Peller, L. "Libidinal Phases, Ego Development, and Play." *Psychoanalytic Study of the Child,* New York: International Universities Press, 1954, Vol. IX, pp. 178-198. An important article detailing children's play from the developmental point of view. Must reading for an increased understanding of the psychoanalytic theory of play.

Piaget, J. *Play, Dreams, and Imitation in Childhood*. New York: W.W. Norton, Co., 1951. The primary source of Piaget's theory of play. Like most of Piaget's writings it requires several readings to be fully assimilated.

Waelder, R. "The Psychoanalytic Theory of Play." *Psychoanalytic Quarterly*, 1933, 2, pp. 208-224. The basic psychoanalytic statement about play.

Winnicott, D.W. *Playing and Reality*. New York: Basic Books, 1971. An excellent though somewhat technical book that contains a restatement of Winnicott's important psychoanalytic concept of the "transitional object."

VI.

CHILD ABUSE: A Complex Case of Mis-socialization

By Jessica Henderson Daniel

For some time, Dr. Benjamin Spock has been the primary authority on child-rearing practices for a large segment of middle America. He remains for many parents and parents-to-be the expert on how to live effectively with growing children. Dr. Spock's best-seller, *Baby and Child Care,* has been joined by numerous other books for parents: Gordon's *Parent Effectiveness Training;* Fitzhugh Dodson's *How to Parent* and *How to Father;* and Rudolf Dreikur's *A Parent's Guide to Child Discipline, Coping with Children's Misbehaviour,* and *The Challenge of Child Training.* Now there are books written specifically for the parents of black children: Phyliss Harrison-Ross and Barbara Wyden's *The Black Child-A Parents' Guide* and James Comer and Alvin Poussaint's *Black Child Care.* Child-rearing experts and parents have acknowledged the need for child development information, as well as suggestions on how to enhance the quality of the parent-child relationship.

A decade ago, the federal government launched a nation-wide program to prepare, more specifically to socialize, the economically disadvantaged child so as to increase his chances for success in school, and help him become a contributing part of mainstream America. Considerable time, energy, and thought have been expended in an effort to design a comprehensive program to meet the social, psychological (often cognitive), and medical needs of Head Start Children, with the explicit assumption that these have some bearing on the developmental process. The federal government, in partnership with local education agencies, has shown interest in the socialization of a large segment of the nation's children in programs such as Head Start.

Socialization refers to "the process by which the individual becomes a member of his social group through acquisition of the group's values, motives and behaviors," and develops to his full potential. Investigators have attempted to improve the process, often to accelerate it where developmental lags may have occurred.

The Problem of Mis-Socialization

More recently, the federal government has focused on the mis-socialization of the child, primarily child abuse and neglect. Mis-socialization refers to a breakdown in the process of an individual becoming a fully-developed member of the group, and a failure to realize his full potential. The Child Abuse Prevention and Treatment Act of 1973, or the Mondale Bill (named after one of the principal sponsors), established a National Center on Child Abuse and Neglect in the Office of Child Development (Department of Health, Education and Welfare). It made available research and funds in order to understand better the children, parents, and families where abuse and neglect were identified.

The literature on child abuse and other related areas of mis-socialization has increased enormously in recent years. Books include Ray Helfer and Henry Kempe's *The Battered Child,* which was for some time the major work in the field, along with David Gil's *Violence Against Children,* Helfer and Kempe's *Helping the Battered Child and His Family,* Susan Steinmetz and Murray Straus' *Violence in The Family,* and David Bakan's *Slaughter of the Innocents.* Andrew Billingsley and Jeanne Giovannoni's *Children of the Storm* concentrates on the black child and protective services, past and present. (Protective services are specialized social services for abusive and neglectful families.) Published articles and research reports are numerous and many more can be expected from currently funded research projects.

Child abuse is not a simple case of a caretaker beating, mutilating or murdering a child. It involves the caretaker and the child in a social context. Many people and institutions become involved with this highly emotional issue: the legislatures (on the federal and state levels) that write the child welfare laws and bills; the "administrative" branches of the federal and state governments, responsible for implementing rules and regulations based on the legislation; the judicial branch whose lawyers and judges actively participate in decision-making concerning the legal and physical custody of children; the police department that can and does become involved with domestic disputes and child abuse cases (the latter two are sometimes inextricably related); the hospital, more specifically the emergency wing, whose doctors, nurses and social workers are often the first professionals having contact with the child and his family; social service agencies, both public and private, whose social workers offer services to the family and, upon request, conduct court investigations of the families; and finally, researchers from the academic community, medical institutions, and social agencies who are interested in learning more about abuse. This list is far from exhaustive, but it includes the major figures in the field.

There are presently two related emphases in child abuse work: clinical practice and research. Clinical practice includes the definition of child abuse, the reporting process, the case management procedures used with families identified, and the development of prevention and treatment programs. Research includes incidence data, the determination of estimated incidence, causal factors or patterns of causal factors associated with child abuse, and the evaluation of screening and intervention programs. Obviously these are closely related since the definition of child abuse and the reporting process clearly determine subjects included in the various research and demonstration projects.

This discussion will be divided into three sections. The first will include definitions, a brief historical sketch, and data on the incidence of child abuse. The second will review causal factors, and include the socio-demographic characteristics of persons who have been reported as the abuser and the abused, plus psychological factors associated with abuse. The third section will describe the reporting process and its implications for certain segments of the population, as well as case management procedures and intervention programs and services.

Child Abuse: Definitions, Background, and Incidence

The problem of defining child abuse reflects the complexity of this social phenomenon. In a classic article that appeared in a 1962 edition of the *Journal of the American Medical Association,* Henry Kempe and others generated interest in abused children with the term "the battered child syndrome." The term is frequently used by physicians and other allied medical professionals when they speak of child abuse. At that time, Kempe defined it as "a term used by us to characterize a clinical condition in young children who have received serious physical abuse, generally from a parent or a foster parent." This definition emphasizes injury as a result of physical abuse. Kempe and others have elaborated on this definition. A more general description is "an illness, with or without inflicted injury, stemming from situations in his home setting which threatens a child's survival." This definition emphasizes the total social context of the child's life. The child does not necessarily have to sustain an injury to be considered in danger. His home setting may be judged to be inadequate for providing protection.

According to the Child Abuse Prevention and Treatment Act of 1973 (federal), child abuse and neglect means "the physical or mental injury, sexual abuse, negligent treatment, or maltreatment of a child under the age of eighteen by a person who is responsible for the child's welfare under circumstances which indicate that the child's health or welfare is threatened by them."

This more inclusive and general definition introduces new terms that raise many questions. What is mental injury? Could a group of mental health workers reach a consensus on definition as well as diagnosis on a given case? The question remains generally unanswered and accounts for the lack of emphasis on mental or psychological abuse. What constitutes "negligent treatment" of a child short of abandonment? Would professionals be able to agree on a definition, description and diagnosis across socio-economic and cultural groups? What is "maltreatment" of the child? Can the use of disciplinary procedures, especially some forms of corporal punishment, be called "maltreatment" of the child?

This definition also introduces neglect of a child, a condition that protective services workers (specialized social workers) see far more frequently than abuse. But there are different kinds of neglect and its causes and results vary considerably. Neglect implies omission. In the case of child neglect it could be purposeful or deliberate omission, omission due to limited financial resources, or omission due to a lack of capacity to love or care.

Most state child abuse laws acknowledge the impact of poverty on the neglect of children. Limited financial resources may be reflected in a child who appears neglected due to inadequate clothing, shelter, diet and medical care. This might suggest poor household management on the part of the parents. It might be an index of society's neglect of its children rather than individual parental neglect, especially when the family lacks the financial capacity to meet the basic needs of the child. In contrast, a child who is adequately dressed, well-nourished, and has a history of good medical care may be neglected. This neglect may be reflected in behavior that indicates a lack or loss of love. Neglect, broadly defined, has no social class boundaries, but neglect among the poor is more visible.

David Gil, who conducted the most comprehensive study of child abuse to date, has his own tentative definition of child abuse: "Physical abuse of children that is intentional, non-accidental use of force, or in tentional, non-accidental acts of omission, on the part of a parent or other caretaker in interaction with a child in his care, aimed at hurting, injuring, or destroying that child." Gil's definition has a "neglect" component that accounts for acts of omission as well as acts of commission. But most important Gil's definition introduced the notion of non-accidental acts.

What are accidents in a pediatric medical setting? Included under this heading are: "falls, fractures, lacerations, automobile accidents, bumps, burns, bruises, dislocations, drownings, head injuries, contusions and crushing injuries, sprains and strains and other injuries and trauma." These accidents are the major causes of death in 1- to 14-year-old children. Research data suggest that families under considerable stress experience more childhood accidents than families under less stress. Child abuse and familial stress have been found to be associated.

It is interesting that the physical symptoms of the child abuse are the same as accidents. When presented with a child with one of the above injuries, how does one determine whether it was caused by an accident or abuse? Particularly in cases that fall into "gray areas," the person making the diagnosis has to use clinical judgment based upon the available data. The nature of the injuries and how the parents and child interact contribute to the determination of the diagnosis, along with the explanation presented. One can assume that there is sometimes a thin line between child abuse and accidents.

To summarize, the definition of child abuse remains unclear due to a lack of consensus around key issues. Does one deal with the physical condition of the child or his total environment? Should clinicians cling to the "battered child syndrome" definition which excludes the social environment of the child? How accurately can the thin line between abuse and accidents be diagnosed? Does the emphasis on physical injury neglect some crucial mental health factors? To what extent is neglect an important contributing factor to abuse? And finally, is it possible to predict abuse, and then act on that prediction? The latter depends upon the extent to which factors associated with abuse can be determined prior to actual abuse.

Defining child abuse is not a minor matter since it determines in part who is identified as abusive. The definition also influences the incidence data and the generation of causal factors associated with child abuse since researchers rely heavily on reported cases as a data source.

Attempts to define child abuse lead to a consideration of two additional questions: is it a recent phenomenon, and what is its scope? Historical reviews indicate that child abuse has a history that is perhaps as old as man. S.V. Radbill's *The History of Child Abuse and Infanticide* traces how children have been treated by adults and society in general. In past centuries children were beaten to drive out the devil. Parents, teachers and ministers believed that the cure-all for the foolishness in the heart of the child was the use of the rod to exorcise it. The industrial revolution contributed significantly to the abuse of children and to their increased mortality. The quality of life for some children bordered on slavery. It is reported that children as young as five years of age were forced to work up to 16 hours a day. The chimney sweep stands out as the "most forlorn waif" of the cities at that time. They were subjected to much brutality at the hands of their masters. Child abuse in work settings continues today among migrant children and children who live near farms and plantations. Their well being affected by owners whose harvests are more important than the health of the children.

There is also a history of "child advocacy," attempts to bring about reform by a segment of society advocating humane treatment of children. It has resulted in some periodic abatement of maltreatment. In this country, the founding of the Society for Prevention of Cruelty to Children in 1871, resulted from a case involving a child in New York City who had been severely mistreated by her adoptive parents. She had been "beaten regularly and was seriously malnourished." Local authorities even when presented with the data, were not convinced that it was appropriate to take legal action against the parents. Interested persons were persistent in their efforts to help Mary Ellen and finally appealed to The Society for the Prevention of Cruelty to Animals (SPCA), which immediately took action. She was removed from the home of her adoptive parents "on the grounds that she was a member of the animal kingdom and that therefore her case could be included under the laws against animal cruelty." The rights of animals have been acknowledged and protected much longer than those of children. The passage of child abuse legislation by the States is a very recent phenomenon.

Data on the incidence of child abuse was first collected during the 1960s. Gil estimates a range of 2.5 to 4.1 million cases. In a 1973 Harvard Educational Review article, Richard Light estimates the annual incidence of child abuse as over half a million. Two other estimates have been published. Stephen Cohen and Allan Sussman estimate 41,000 cases (based on actual samples of the 10 most populous states and projections to the national population) and Saad Nagi estimates 925,000 reportable cases. Of the latter, two thirds were actually reported and of these, over half were substantiated. The Nagi estimate is based on a nation-wide survey of agencies and programs involved with abuse and neglect.

There are serious problems, however. Saad Nagi and Richard Light both raised the issue of "false positives," that is, persons identified as abusive but who really are not. "False negatives," or cases of abuse not reported are also noteworthy. Combined with the lack of consensus around definition, both false positives and false negatives only add to the difficulties faced by those responsible for compiling incidence data.

Aggressive reporting programs are under way in some states. These programs are useful, but also produce a high rate of "false positives." The state of Florida has a public awareness campaign centered on the child abuse issue. It is generating considerable interest. There are statewide toll-free telephone numbers for reporting cases of abuse and neglect. During the period beginning October 1972 through September 1973, over 29,000 abuse and neglect cases were reported. Of these about 60 percent were subsequently substantiated, meaning over 10,000 cases were "false positives," no small number.

Causal Factors: The Abuser and the Abused

Causal Factors associated with child abuse generally fall into two conceptual models: the psychiatric and sociological/social psychological. Sources of information include formal research findings as well as clinical observations.

The Psychiatric Model

This model focuses on the parent or caretaker as the primary causal factor in child abuse. The parent or caretaker is seen as having serious mental problems that cause abuse to the child. Clinical interviews and psychological tests are sources of data used to determine the nature and extent of the mental problems. Yet one can question the validity of such interviews and tests. Test samples are frequently small and often the findings are tentative and not generalizable to a larger population. Causes cited tend to be clearly inconsistent and contradictory. For example, one article stated that the abusing parent was a psychopath and then stated that the child abuser is no different from the rest of society.

One commonly stated "fact" is that persons who abuse their children were often abused as children themselves. But what does this mean? Does it mean that they were spanked or severely beaten or maltreated with or without physical contact? Who defined abuse, the parent or the researchers? The psychiatric model has minimal support. Few parents have been found to be seriously disturbed and in need of psychotherapy or long term psychiatric treatment. Yet the model remains popular for those who see child abuse as a case of a "sick" parent destroying a child.

The Sociological and Social Psychological Models

These two models have attempted to provide the demographic characteristics of persons who have been reported as abusive parents and describe how the interaction of the individuals (parents and child) in a social context may contribute to child abuse. David Gil's study, using one model, was based upon a nationwide survey of reported cases of child abuse in 1967-1968. It represents the most extensive data collection and has yielded the most comprehensive demographic data. He found that the reporting rates for nonwhite chidren were over three times that for whites. More specifically, per 100,000, the rate of reporting for whites was 6.7 while it was 21.0 for nonwhites. Over 61 percent of the perpetrators were of minority group status and over 52 percent of them had been previously abusive.

Severity of injuries was related to ethnicity. Thirty-five and two tenths percent of the white children's injuries were considered serious as compared with 52.2 percent of the Negro and Puerto Rican children. Severe injuries were more likely to have been inflicted by persons under the age of 25 and by women, especially single women. A high proportion of families with female heads of household were reported as abusive. Non-white households had a greater representation in this category. Child-abusing parents tended to be less educated and the male parents had a high unemployment rate. Over one third of the families were receiving some public assistance, and over one half had received public assistance at one time.

Gil attributes this over-representation of non-whites to "the higher incidence of poverty and poverty-related social and psychological deviance, and to the higher rate of fatherless homes and large families among the non-white population segments, all of which were found to be strongly associated with child abuse." He went on to describe differences in child-rearing practices and pointed out that non-whites tended to be more physical in their punishment styles.

Based on the Gil data, one could easily conclude that there is a cause-effect relationship between child abuse and poverty/minority group status. However, this issue of reporting bias cannot be ignored. Gil has acknowledged this problem. There are reasons to believe that there is selective reporting of child abuse cases. The records used in the Gil study came from the Department of Public Welfare and the police department, two agencies that are closely associated with the poor and members of minority groups. The case reports (the source of the records) came from public hospitals that serve segments of the population that lack the financial resources necessary to utilize the services of the private practitioner. The latter has been found to be less likely to report cases of child abuse. The reporting process will be discussed in the last section of this chapter.

In addition to the disproportionate number of poor and minority group status families, the number of households headed by a female is notable. A recent review of the fatherless family research data indicates that these families are poor in part because of the salary discrepancy between males and females. Also, marital discord increases with financial problems. It's likely that financial difficulties existed before the father was no longer present. It is significant that many adult males were unemployed.

Another factor associated with child abuse, and often related to poverty, is family size. Families where abuse has occurred tend to have four or more children, which is larger than the national average. It has been suggested that the abused child may be an unwanted or unplanned child.

David Gil probably emerges as the key proponent of the sociological position. He sees child abuse as an extension of a society that recommends violence and physical aggression as a way to resolve conflict. There is no doubt that our society is violent. It is reflected in the murder statistics that continue to climb year after year. Even more disturbing is the fact that one is more likely to be murdered by a friend or relative than by a stranger. Is child abuse so different? Some have pointed to the association between familial violence and child abuse in presenting their arguments against corporal punishment; a familiar part of disciplinary procedures in this country regardless of social class and race. It is argued that the use of corporal punishment increases the probability of additional violence.

Stress has been identified as a causal factor associated with child abuse. The various social classes and racial/ethnic groups experience different kinds of stress that may culminate in the abuse of children. One's socio-economic status and ethnic identification often determine what opportunities are open to an individual and a family. They can determine living circumstances, access to helping services, and the relationship of institutions to the family. Job related problems can generate stress in the caretakers' lives. Problems include unemployment, underemployment, or stress on the job. The latter may be a function of competition. High mobility may contribute to familial stress. Many families move every few years due to job relocations. One result is often considerable isolation between a family and persons who could offer support during times of crisis.

The Abused

Early studies concentrated on the parent as the causal factor in cases of child abuse, but more recently the child's involvement has also been studied. Such studies should help determine, among other things, why one child is subject to abuse, while other children in the same family are not.

The child's temperament and learned behavior patterns may increase vulnerability to abuse. It is clear that new-born infants place new pressures and demands on their parents. If there is a mismatching of a child and caretaker in terms of expectations and temperament, the relationship may become strained and could lead to abuse. For example, a mother who prefers a quiet, passive baby, but who has, instead, an active demanding baby who consumes a considerable amount of her time and energy is more likely to be abusive. A child whose physical appearance creates problems for the parent may be vulnerable. A sickly, weak child does not meet the expectations of the parents, and may contribute to the frustration of the parent who does not want to be seen with such a child. Children who have been treated harshly develop behavior patterns that differ from those who have been treated more kindly. The behavior patterns of the former often make them difficult to manage. Some children discover that only misbehavior will generate interest and attention, and although the attention is negative, misbehavior becomes their learned pattern of interaction. This pattern can generalize from parents to others so that it becomes an integral part of the child's interaction. He is thus likely to be abused even by those who are not normally abusive toward children.

The Gil data indicate that these children have particular characteristics that warrant further study. Well over one half of the abused children in his study had been previously abused, and were found to have some emotional and intellectual problems. It may be difficult to determine cause and effect in this instance. Did the abuse cause the problems or did the problems play a role in causing the abuse? While there is a need for more research on how the child may contribute to the likelihood of his being abused, related data indicate that abusive behavior is not limited to a parent acting in an isolated social setting. It is likely that the physical and psychological characteristics of the child in a particular social setting contribute to the situation.

Case Studies: Reporting, Management, and Services

Since hospitals are usually perceived by parents as institutions that provide help, it is not unusual for concerned parents to bring their children, with and without physical injuries, to an emergency room or to their regular medical caretaker for assistance. (Cases also come to the attention of the police, fire department, and social service agencies.) The following are three cases that were presented in the emergency room of an urban hospital.

Case I

A black teen-age mother of two small children, (a 2½-year-old female and a 3-month male), brought her son to the hospital saying that the child "moves funny." She lived on AFDC (Assistance for Dependent Children) with her children in her own apartment. The child was examined and found to have a new leg fracture and an old arm fracture. When confronted with these findings, the mother could not offer an explanation for either the old or new injuries. The child was admitted to the hospital while more information was obtained from the mother and from community agencies that had been involved with her.

The mother subsequently presented the following explanation for the injuries. At night her daughter often gets out of bed and sometimes picks up the baby, even though she has been told not to. The mother explained that her daughter may have dropped the baby as she tried to place him back in the car-bed, his bed in lieu of a crib which the welfare department had yet to deliver.

At a case conference, the hospital social worker reported that the mother's family had a history of alcoholism and violence. The mother had run away from home on several occasions, and dropped out of school after completing the ninth grade. The hospital staff judged the mother as hostile, due in part to her many questions and her assertions of "knowing her rights." But the community agency presented the mother as very bright and articulate. She had a history of taking good care of her two children, including keeping well baby clinic appointments at the neighborhood health center where she was also an active member of a mother's group. Both children were reported as being well-stimulated and nurtured.

The case was reported to the department of public welfare as a case of child abuse/neglect. But was it? What evidence did the hospital staff respond to? How plausible was the mother's story? What impact did the mother's perceived hostility and aggression have on the decision to hospitalize? The reader can decide.

Case II

One evening a young white couple appeared in the hospital emergency room with an 8-month-old male baby who had sustained head injuries and a chest bruise. The father explained that he had placed the child on the floor in their studio apartment while he turned his back to get something. In the short period of two or three minutes, the baby had managed to pick up a hammer and subsequently drop it on his head and then his chest. While the father had not seen these events, he felt quite strongly that this is how the injuries occurred. The mother had not been in the apartment at the time and was unable to verify the story. The father, fearing that hospital personnel doubted his story, and probably suspected that he had abused the child, provided data he hoped would minimize the possibility of being identified as an abusive parent. He also tried to elicit sympathy for himself by relating a series of illnesses which accounted for his current unemployment status. The mother was described as an ineffectual person who said little. In discussing the development of the child, she indicated that he ate solids and vocalized age-appropriately. The family had recently moved to the state and had just applied for welfare. The baby was admitted to the hospital for observation and to allow some time for an evaluation of the parents.

The hospital personnel noted that the parents visited the child infrequently and their interactions with him appeared awkward, as though they were not sure what to do. The baby did not know how to eat with a spoon, meaning that he had probably been bottle-fed and perhaps not introduced to solid foods. The baby did not vocalize at all; another contradiction of the mother's earlier assertions.

A home visit by a social worker yielded worrisome data about the mental health of the parents. The father found it diffucult to focus on a given topic and could not, on occasion, discriminate between fact and fantasy. The mother's psychological well-being was questionable too, in that she appeared to agree with the father's explanations and information, although they were inconsistent and contradictory.

The case was reported as a case of child abuse/neglect. Should the child be returned to the parents? Why? Why not? What services should be offered to the parents?

Case III

A young white mother brought her 6-month-old son to the emergency room. She was bright, articulate and well-dressed. Her son had sustained a head injury as a result of her leaving him unattended momentarily on a changing table while she went to get something. He had fallen off the table and hit his head. The child's medical record indicated that some six weeks earlier the mother had brought the child to the emergency room with similar injuries and had related the same story. Was this a pattern of "accidents" that needed investigation?

A social work interviewer described the mother as a very bright woman who had terminated her career plans to marry a professional man and begin a family. The mother resented her husband being able to pursue his career and resented her child, whose presence not only meant an end (permanent or temporary) to her career plans, but also isolated her in a distant suburb.

Was this a case of neglect? What services should be offered to this frustrated mother?

The Reporting Process

Persons responsible for reporting cases of child abuse and neglect are indicated in the various state child abuse laws. In all states, physicians are required to report cases of abuse. Nurses are required to report in 34 states, social workers in 25 states, teachers in 24 states, and police officers in 9 states. All states allow for citizens' reports. Persons who report are generally immune from libel and slander suits, since it is assumed that they are reporting in good faith and no malice is intended. Reports are filed with the state agency responsible for abuse and neglect cases. In most states, it is the welfare department.

But there is clear evidence that a substantial number of child abuse cases go unreported, even though they are seen and sometimes treated by persons required to report. Quite often those required to report are close to the family and feel some loyalty to the parents. Massachusetts survey data imply that physicians, especially those in private practice, see cases of abuse but fail to report them. This may account for an underreporting of middle and upper income families.

One reason people fail to report is that they have serious concerns about what will happen to the family as a unit and to the individual family members. A child who is considered to be in immediate danger may be removed from the home environment. But if the family's problems associated with the abuse can be treated, and the environmental factors which precipitated the abuse are removed or minimized, the child may remain with the family.

How likely is it that parents and children will receive help? Generally, the department of public welfare is the agency that receives reports of child abuse. This is an agency that often provides poor services to poor people due to inadequate funding and high staff turnover. The truth is that the parents and children may not receive needed services.

The family may or may not be involved with the courts. The thought of court can be overwhelming, since many persons have had little or no court experience, and often have no legal help to turn to. The decision of the court may involve the physical custody of the child on a temporary or permanent basis. The judge may also require that services be made available to the family. In any event, the family may attend a series of hearings over a period of one year while the court decides whether the case should be dropped (child returned home without contact with the welfare department) or the state should take custody of the child.

When a child is removed from the home, what happens to him? If an acceptable relative is readily available, the child will probably be sent there. If not, he will be placed in a foster home or a residential center. In any event, the child will experience some loss of family ties and will need a period of orientation. The length of the separation may interfere with the bond between parent and child, particularly in the case of a younger child. On the other hand, it may facilitate the child's capacity to develop bonds, especially if the natural parent has not been a comforting figure.

The length of time the child remains separated from his parents varies. Records show that the child will move several times during the separation. Parents can often visit the child but not always. What does all this mean to the child and the family unit? It often means disorganization and the generation of a great deal of anger, frustration, and despair.

Will the child be evaluated and subsequently receive services? The data (Governor's Commission on Adoption and Foster Care) indicate that approximately half of the evaluations requested will actually be conducted. Of those only half will be found to be in need of treatment.

Will the family receive services and how long will they be continued? Many protective cases both in public and private agencies are carried to a maximum of nine months. This is usually not enough time, but there are too many others to be treated and too few staff members.

What kind of record is kept on abusive parents and their children?

State child abuse registries are often a target of controversy. The costs and benefits, fiscal and human, of the registries generate heated discussions on the part of concerned professionals and citizens. Other issues include whether suspected and/or proven cases of abuse are to be included, what sort of information is recorded, who has access to registry information, and what safeguards are employed, to mention a few.

All of the above factors contribute to indecision and inaction on the part of those responsible for reporting child abuse. Until reporting is accepted as beneficial to the family, a great many cases will remain unreported.

The Case Management Process

The lack of agreement on definitions has made it difficult to determine whether or not a parent is abusive. Much depends on how data are collected and evaluated. Case conferences are one means used to elicit information and plan dispositions.

At case conferences, persons known to have had contacts with the family are invited to share their knowledge. The case conference chairman, with the help of persons present, then decides whether or not the child has been abused and if so, what should happen to the parents and child. There is considerable variability in the quality and quantity of data available. The amount of time between the "identification" of the case and the case conference can vary widely. In a case where a child will be a long-term hospital patient, the data collection can be more systematic, as opposed to an out-patient or social admission where a sense of urgency in making a decision about the family can hinder proper disposition.

The interpretation of the data depends greatly upon the professional, racial, and ethnic case conference group. Persons with experience and varying backgrounds often provide the balance needed to put the data into proper perspective and provide safeguards against biased interpretation of the data. Decision-making processes must be examined carefully. More specifically, are decisions based on the data, on the absence of "needed" date, or in spite of the data?

Services

Some feel that removing the child from the home is effective since it separates the child from the abusive parent. But since it is agreed that the causes of abuse are far more involved, other intervention methods may be indicated. It has been suggested that "services should be able to respond creatively to individual families' problems with services suited to their needs'' as opposed to families having to fit their needs to the services available.

The following are possible services and intervention programs: social work counseling, which can include the coordination of other services to the family; medical-dental evaluation of the family with treatment where necessary; family advocacy which not only attempts to secure services for the family but provides instruction for clients and institutions to facilitate future contacts between the two; parent groups which offer child development information and support for parents; psychiatric and psychological evaluation and treatment where necessary for parents and child; child care, full-time and part-time; legal services; foster care for the child; home-maker services to help parents organize and maintain a household; emergency services such as hot-lines where people can call for assistance; and crisis centers where entire families can stay on a temporary basis. All these should act to strengthen the family and increase its capacity to nurture and protect the child.

Conclusions

Both research and clinical practice suggest that child abuse is a complex case of mis-socialization that involves not just a caretaker and child but a complex variety of persons and issues. It has become a concern of the general citizenry, but prospective parents and prospective teachers have a particular vested interest in the social problem. They have the primary responsibility for providing environments which foster the healthy development of the child. It is important that they be attuned to this problem, especially to the potential detrimental and retarding effects it can have on the development of the child. It is crucial that they also be aware of the process and consequences of being "officially identified" or reported as an abusive family, so that, in the case of parents, they can be prepared themselves and in the case of teachers, they can prepare others.

Parents can acknowledge that given a certain social-psychological context, child abuse can become a possibility in their family. The research data on factors associated with child abuse, while inconclusive, describe stresses and circumstances that might produce a break-down in the parent-child relationship. An awareness may help parents seek assistance before rather than after the fact.

Teachers, as both transmitters of knowledge and as advocates for the total development of the child need to be alert to indication of abuse. Children who have been abused may need protection from additional abuse. The families and children may be able to utilize services. The teacher may serve as a first-line advocate, contacting the service structure within the school system. Some abused children are provocative and may test teachers constantly. Being sensitive to this problem may better help professionals manage their behavior and others so as to decrease the likelihood of additional abuse at school.

While there are many issues and problems associated with child abuse, responsible and sensitive awareness may result in the protection of more children and the strengthening of more families.

REFERENCES

Daniel, J. H. "Child Abuse and the Vulnerable Black Family." Paper presented at meeting of Association of Black Psychologists, Boston, August 1975. Discussion of vulnerability of black family, i.e., identification as being abusive and involvement with the courts.

Daniel, J. H. and Hyde, J. N. "Working with High-Risk Families." Family Advocacy and Parent Education Program. *Children Today.* November-December 1975. Descriptions of service programs associated with a research project investigating social pediatric illnesses.

Erlanger, H. B. "Social Class and Corporal Punishment in Childrearing: A Reassessment." *American Sociological Review,* February 1974. Corporal punishment is found to exist at all social class levels.

Gelles, R. "Child Abuse as Psychopathology: A Sociological Critique and Reformulation." *American Journal of Orthopsychiatry,* July 1973. A critical review of the psychiatric model of causal factors associated with child abuse.

Gil, D. "Violence against Children." *Journal of Marriage and the Family.* November 1971. A presentation of child abuse survey data.

Gruber, A. R. "Report—Massachusetts Governor's Commission on Adoption and Foster Care, 1973." A follow-up description of foster children and the status of adoption in one state.

Helfer, R. and Kempe, C. H. (Editors). *The Battered Child.* Chicago: University of Chicago Press, 1974. A review of research and clinical data on abusive families.

_____. *Helping the Battered Child and His Family.* Philadelphia: J. B. Lippincott Co., 1972. A handbook for clinicians who work with abusive and neglectful parents.

Kempe, C. H., Silverman, F. N., Steele, B. F., Droegemueller, W., and Silver, H. R. "The Battered Child Syndrome." *Journal of the American Medical Association,* 181, 1962. A classic paper in the field.

Light, R. "Abused and Neglected Children in American: A Study of Alternative Policies." *Harvard Educational Review, 1973,* 43. A re-analysis of the Gil data and mis-identification issues, i.e., false positives and false negatives.

Nagi, S. Z. "Child Abuse and Neglect Programs: A National Review." *Children Today,* May-June 1975, 4. Incidence data from several sources.

Newberger, E. H., Hass, G., and Mulford, R. "Child Abuse in Massachusetts." *Massachusetts Physician,* 1973, 4. Survey of pediatricians in the state.

Newberger, E. H. and Hyde, J. N. "Child Abuse: Principles and Implications of Current Pediatric Practices." *Pediatric Clinics of North America,* August 1975. A review of child abuse literature as it relates to practice.

Newberger, E. H., Reed, R. B., Daniel, J. H., Hyde, J. N., and Kotelchuck, M. "Toward an Etiologic Classification of Pediatric Social Illness." Paper presented at the meeting of the Society for Research in Child Development, Denver, April 1975. A descriptive epidemiology of child abuse and neglect, failure to thrive, accidents and poisonings of children under four years of age.

This work was supported in part by a grant from the Office of Child Development, Department of Health, Education & Welfare. (Project OCD-CB-141).

VII.

MORAL EDUCATION IN EARLY CHILDHOOD

By John S. Dacey

✳ The moral development of children was once the main educational
objective of our schools. The first schools in America were closely allied
to religious groups in sponsorship and curriculum. The school marm and
master were expected to inculcate good character in their students by any
means they could. There was no real question as to the definition of
morality in the rural communities of seventeenth, eighteenth and nine-
teenth century America. True, there were theological differences, but
almost all persons of responsibility in the town embraced basically the
same ethical beliefs and helped to reinforce these beliefs in the young.

At the turn of the century, unanimity as to ethical principles began
to disintegrate. The causes of this discord are difficult to pinpoint, but
the waves of immigration, together with spiralling urbanization and in-
dustrialization surely played a major part. The so-called "melting pot"
provided for greater disparity of opinion on ethical principles.

The role of the schools in character development shrank smaller and
smaller. Teachers were admonished to avoid moralizing,
propagandizing, indoctrinating. Democracy was seen as guaranteeing
each person's right to his own set of values, which schools were forbidden to mold. The last vestige of religiosity was removed in the 1950s
when Madeleine Murray won her Supreme Court case against praying in
school.

It is interesting to note that the situation in the Soviet Union over the past 75 years has been just the opposite. Viewing the education of youth as the crucial factor in the future success of the U.S.S.R., Soviet educators have increasingly refined their techniques for conditioning morality. In fact, the most important aspect of Soviet education, *vospitania,* translates *moral education.* The Soviet approach consists mainly of conditioning *habits* of morality. "Moral education should begin very early, before the child completes his first year, and before he can understand the nature of adult explanation," states T. A. Repin, writing in *From Zero to Seven (Ot Nolya do Semi,* 1967, p. 154). If conditioning is done well, he argues, understanding will come later. Repin feels that a high level of accord between teachers and parents on ethical principles is absolutely essential in moral education. In terms of mutual agreement on a moral code, therefore, the Soviet Union appears to be where the United States was at the turn of the century.

Americans today are experiencing a rebirth of interest in moral education. This movement predominates at the elementary and junior high levels, but is rapidly gaining ground at the pre-school level. Proponents say that Watergate, our high crime rate, and the "identity crisis" of our disaffected youth indicate the need to assist the child toward a well thought out value system which can guide his actions. This renewed interest is not based on a revival of religion, however. Its proponents argue that most Americans (and, indeed, most human beings) still subscribe to a unified moral code, which is not derived from any religion, but from our mutual need to interact fairly with each other. They believe that children tend to proceed through a series of stages to a full acceptance of this code and that education should systematically promote this natural development. They urge that teachers no longer restrict efforts to educate their pupils in a body of factual information and skills. As Niblett puts it:

> A technical knowledge of, say navigation can be immensely interesting in itself. But the course the ship is to take is chosen for quite other reasons than the navigator's skill in plotting it. The educated man needs to discuss his direction of progress and the "why's" of conduct as well as to build up knowledge and skills (Niblett, 1963, p. 27).

The research of several highly respected psychologists lends evidence to this point of view. This chapter will consider the work of psychologists Jean Piaget and Lawrence Kohlberg on moral development and of Kohlberg, Louis Raths, Sidney Simon, and their associates on moral education. Although this book concentrates on early childhood, it is necessary to a clear understanding of these theories that the full developmental sequence be described. The chapter concludes with examples of methods of clarifying values especially designed for the early childhood years.

Piaget's Theory of Moral Development

Jean Piaget is best known for his theory of cognitive development. Director of the Institute J. J. Rousseau in Geneva, Switzerland, he has written nearly 50 books on this aspect of human intelligence. His ideas on the moral judgment of the child, first presented in 1932, have also received widespread acclaim.

Piaget defines morality as "the understanding of and adherence to rules through one's own volition." He has studied the development of this process in a number of ways but his main technique has been through watching children of various ages play the game of marbles. The game calls for each competitor to shoot a marble from behind a line into a circle of other marbles. Any marbles knocked out of the area then belong to the shooter. Piaget believes that this social situation offers a good opportunity for perceiving the development of morality.

His theory divides the development of morality into two categories: practice of the rules and consciousness of the rules. Practice of the rules develops in four stages:

Stage 1. The individual stage (ages 0-3). In this stage the child is trying to understand the nature of the game of marbles, which is a novelty to him. There are regularities in the play of the game. The child tends to ritualize the regularity. He does this until the act is mastered, then he grows weary of it.

The rituals are not yet rules; there is no "oughtness" attached. The marbles are representative of this stage of morality in that they are symbols to be played with. They can stand for something else, e.g., they can be cooked, they can be eggs in a nest, etc. These symbols are what Piaget calls "played" symbols. Only with the development of language and imagery can these symbols become objects of thought in themselves. Through practice and experience, one thing comes to stand for another.

The sense of obligation to follow rituals, which then become rules, comes only when some other person intervenes. If the intervener is respected and requests that a ritual be followed, then a sense of obligation comes into being.

Stage 2. The egocentric stage (ages 4-7). By now the older children have taught the younger ones the rules of marbles. Of course, just watching older kids, and sometimes instructions from parents, lead to knowledge of the rules, too. Children at this age try hard to follow the rules, but make many mistakes. The importance of the game is that you play it with others.

In this stage, children not only misunderstand rules, but they often interpret them differently from each other. In other words, they play according to different sets of rules. The main aspect of this stage is that they don't seem to *mind* that there are different criteria for each player. It is perfectly all right with them if everybody wins. The goal is imitation of the older, more prestigious children.

Stage 3. Cooperation (ages 8-11). Now there is a general will to discover rules which are fixed and common for all players. Everyone must play the same. However, there are still considerable discrepancies in the child's information. The main point of this stage is no longer the manual dexterity of knocking a marble out of the circle. It has become winning out over another person, within the context of complicated rules. The game has now become truly social.

This cooperation is only a matter of intention. The child at this age tends to play according to the rules which seem reasonable to him. At best, he will give in to a rule which he doesn't like for the duration of one game only.

Stage 4. Codification of rules (age 12-plus). Previously, the child made many mistakes because he was incapable of reasoning abstractly. He may have noticed inconsistencies but he was unable to alleviate them.

Consistency begins to prevail through the adolescent's new interest in the codification of the rules, a fact of great importance for teachers. Not only do adolescents seek to cooperate, and to sanction the behavior of anyone who doesn't; they also take great pleasure in anticipating *all possible cases* and in codifying them.

Since there are at least 10 known varieties of the game of marbles and many options within each set of rules, the amount of information that the adolescent needs to store in his mind on this minor aspect of his life is astounding. I once spent several days with a group of my teenaged friends, writing out the rules for the game of Black Jack, or "21." It never occurred to us to look them up in a book. We thoroughly enjoyed trying to decide what *we* thought was fair.

The thoroughness with which a child practices rules may or may not indicate his *consciousness* of them. The two are tied together but not rigidly. Piaget argues that there are three stages in the development of consciousness of the rules:

Stage 1. Individualism (ages 0-5). At first, rules are learned subconsciously as interesting examples rather than obligatory reality. When the child approaches any play, he knows that some things are allowed and some are forbidden. He also knows that these warnings are not applicable from time to time only, but are meant to hold with great regularity (e.g., you must *never* rip a newspaper into shreds). At the end of this stage the child develops a sense of "oughtness", but his specific understanding of the rules is limited.

Stage 2. Heteronomy (ages 6-9). To get at the consciousness of the rules here, Piaget asks three questions: "Can the rules be changed?"

Have the rules always been the same?" How did the rules begin?"

In answering these questions, Piaget discovered that children become extremely rigid during this stage in terms of their respect for rules. The child believes that rules come from an authority figure, usually his father, but sometimes the mayor of the town, or the governor of the state. He is willing to see the rules changed occasionally, but he believes that if they do change it is because one of the authorities has changed them. Thus, if rules come from paternal authority, they are in essence sacred and unchangeable. To children of this age, what few changes they make to the rules come not from them, but are the discovery of eternal truth.

These attitudes develop from the continuous union between the child's ego and the elders. Just as a mystic cannot differentiate between his ideas and those of God, the child cannot distinguish between his own rule changes and the rules imposed upon him from above.

Stage 3. Autonomy (ages 10-12). Now the rules become the tools of the player, not the dictates of the adult or the older child. Any change of the rules is permitted so long as all agree on it. Among adolescents, democracy seems to be the natural extension of the earlier theocratic viewpoint. Now there is a natural equality of all participants. Of course, some ideas are more reasonable than others; the child counts on the group to recognize these as such. He also counts on the group not to allow unfair innovations, for these would make the game less a matter of work and skill than it is. An adolescent comes to realize that other generations have made changes in the rules. Marbles, for example, must have started with rounded pebbles with which children amused themselves. Originally, the rules of marbles were invented by the children themselves.

I would argue that Piaget's theory of moral development is an admirable description of development *across* age groups, but I believe it has the weakness of paying too little attention to differences *within* age groups. This has been the significant contribution of psychologist Lawrence Kohlberg.

Kohlberg's Theory of Moral Development

Kohlberg, professor of education and social psychology at Harvard, has studied the development of moral judgment for nearly 20 years. He suggests that three approaches to the study of moral development may be taken.

(1) We can infer the individual's morality from observations of his behavior in situations calling for moral judgment. This is primarily what Piaget has studied.

(2)   We can attempt to determine the amount of guilt that accompanies the person's failure to resist temptation.

(3)   We can ask the person what he thinks should be done in a series of hypothetical situations, and why he thinks so. This has been Kohlberg's method.

Clearly, the three are not necessarily closely related. A person may act according to some standard but not realize it. Conversely, he may say he believes in that standard, but not actually behave that way when we observe him. Kohlberg has found, however, that there is fairly high correlation between the child's hypothetical judgment and his behavior. His technique has the advantage of investigating many situations in a short period of time.

What determines our moral beliefs and behavior? Kohlberg suggests three explanations:

(1)   Freud and his followers in psychoanalysis have argued that the young child develops a conscience, a set of beliefs about morality, based on the ideals presented to him by the adults responsible for him. They refer to this as his "superego." The strength of his superego is said to determine his behavior. However, research has given very little credence to this theory.

(2)   Some religious groups have argued that the conscience is a combination of learned beliefs and innate knowledge of right and wrong. If the child's specific beliefs coincide with his inherited conscience, he will be "good." This theory suffers from the same problem as the psychoanalytic one above: ideals often fail to coincide with behavior.

(3)   Kohlberg's position is that morality is a matter of *decision-making ability* rather than of strength of conscience or superego. This is a function of what Freudians call our "ego." Thus, moral behavior is determined mainly by intelligence, self-esteem, and ability to delay gratification (our so-called "will-power"). Knowledge of consequences (e.g., the odds of getting caught) also plays a large part. Philosophical beliefs, especially children's, tend to have a minor effect on the decision-making process.

However, Kohlberg believes (as does Piaget) that there is an innate aspect in human morality. It does not depend solely on what we have been taught. This innate aspect he calls the "principle of justice". It consists of our understanding that all humans are basically equal in value, and that fairness in our interrelations should be maintained. This principle is a part of our nature and is universal. Rules (e.g., "stop at the red light") differ from culture to culture, but the principle of justice (e.g., the Golden Rule) transcends cultures. When the conditions are appropriate, justice is the natural result of social existence. Adolescents at Piaget's codification stage often typify this need for fairness.

Kohlberg sees the development of moral judgment as an increasingly strong belief in human equality, and of actions in accordance with it. He suggests that this happens in three stages:

(1) *Pre-conventional.* The child is amoral; he acts on self-interest and fear of punishment.

(2) *Conventional.* Concern for conventional rules of society begins, as does regard for authority and judgment of others; the child is group-oriented.

(3) *Post-conventional.* Self-accepted principles come into primacy; emphasis is on morality for its own sake, even if consequences are painful.

A comparison of Kohlberg's stages with Piaget's appears in Figure 4. The comparison is between the kinds of reasoning used, not ages. Kohlberg's stages do not necessarily correspond to any age.

FIGURE 4. A COMPARISON OF PIAGET'S AND KOHLBERG'S STAGES OF MORALITY

Piaget	Kohlberg
S1. Individual	S1. Pre-conventional
S2. Egocentric	S2. Conventional
S3. Cooperation	
S4. Codification	S3. Post-conventional

Each of Kohlberg's three stages are divided into two substages. These substages are presented in Figure 5 (adapted from Kohlberg, 1968). With each is an example of the typical response a child at that substage might make to a hypothetical moral dilemma.

FIGURE 5. KOHLBERG'S STAGES OF MORAL JUDGMENT

The dilemma: Al, age 17, sees his brother Jimmy, age 10, steal money from their mother's purse. Should Al tell Mom what Jimmy did?

STAGE 1. PRE-CONVENTIONAL MORALITY

Substage 1. *Obedience and Punishment.* Child is self-centered, has strict pleasure-pain orientation.
Al: "I wouldn't tell Mom—Jimmy would only get even with me later. It's better not to get involved."

Substage 2. *Naive Instrumental Hedonism.* Trade-offs and deals are made, but only if the child sees something in it for himself. Need for satisfaction is still uppermost, but an awareness of the value of reciprocity has begun.
Al: "It's better if I don't tell. I do bad things sometimes and I wouldn't want Jimmy squealing on me."

STAGE 2. CONVENTIONAL MORALITY

Substage 3. *Good-Boy Morality.* Child is eager for approval of others. Wants to maintain good relations.
Al: "It's better to tell on him. Otherwise, Mom might think I was in on it."

Substage 4. *Authority and Social Order.* Child now seeks approval of society in general, but has rigid ideas as to what rules are; "law and order" mentality.
Al: "I have no choice but to tell. Stealing just isn't right."

STAGE 3. POST-CONVENTIONAL MORALITY

Substage 5. *Contractual Legalistic.* Child makes contracts and tries hard to keep them; attempts to keep from violating the will or rights of others, believes in the common good.
Al: "I'll try to persuade Jimmy to put the money back. If he won't, I'll tell. I hate to do it, but that money belongs to Mom, and he shouldn't have taken it."

Substage 6. *Universal Ethics, Individual Conscience.* Obedience to social rules, except where they can be shown to contradict universal justice; the principles of pacifism, conscientious objection, and civil disobedience fall into this category.
Al: "The most important thing is that Jimmy comes to see he's being unfair to Mom. Telling on him won't help that. I'm going to try to show him why he's wrong, then I'll help him earn money to pay Mom back without her knowing."

Most young children and most delinquents are in Substages 1 and 2. Most adults are in Substages 3 and 4. Kohlberg estimates that 20 to 25 percent of American adults are in the postconventional substages (5 and 6) with only 5 to 10 percent ever reaching Substage 6.

At the lower substages, the person acts to avoid punishment; at the higher stages, he acts to avoid self-condemnation. Conduct, therefore, is correlated with beliefs, with the reasons for the conduct differing greatly at the various levels. Higher level subjects are much less likely to cheat, for example. It is clear that this is because they find cheating inconsistent with their life styles, rather than because they fear discovery.

One interesting experiment investigated the willingness of persons at the six substages to inflict pain on others. The setting for the study was the Milgram electric shock obedience test, in which subjects think they are allowed to administer shock of from 15 to 450 volts to a "learner" in order to get him to learn a task quickly. The "learner" is actually a collaborator who is not really shocked but who puts on a convincing performance. In this experiment, a majority of Stage Six subjects either refused to participate or quit when the victim expressed pain. The majority of the subjects at the other moral levels continued with the experiment. Many of the Stage Five subjects said they wanted to quit but felt they shouldn't because they had agreed to take part.

Kohlberg finds that about 50 percent of an individual's moral statements fall into one dominant substage, and the rest fall into the two adjacent substages. The substage of thinking remains fairly constant regardless of the content of the dilemma. The same substages are also found in other cultures; the sequence of development is the same, although the speed of development is faster and is more likely to proceed to higher levels in some cultures than in others.

In addition to his considerable research on moral development, Kohlberg and his associates have conducted numerous investigations in moral education. The next section describes this work.

Kohlberg's Approach to Moral Education

As was pointed out earlier in this chapter, moral education in the U.S. since the turn of the century has been limited. What there was had virtually ended by the 1930s. The goals then were to explain the American code of ethics to children, exhort them to follow the code, and provide them with activities aimed at practising the code. These efforts were found to be almost entirely ineffective.

Kohlberg and his co-workers have implemented a new approach to moral education which overcomes several important limitations of earlier methods. The Kohlberg technique relies on the universal principle of justice, rather than on cultural mores. It attempts to upgrade moral understanding and behavior through personal experiences rather than through the teacher's exhortations. Finally it depends on carefully researched psychological data, rather than on philosophical speculations.

The approach defines moral education as the stimulation of the next step of development rather than indoctrination of a specific moral code. It is a two-step process:

> (1)   Arousal of genuine moral conflict, uncertainty, and disagreement about genuinely problematic situations...
>
> (2)   The presentation of modes of thought one stage above the child's own.

Most children prefer to function at the highest level of moral reasoning that they can comprehend. This is usually one level above the child's dominant level. Reasoning too far above the child's own level is not understood, and reasoning at lower stages, while understood, is rejected. Adults trying to reason with children often seem to alternate between appeals too advanced for the child to comprehend, or too childish for acceptance.

While there have been no systematic studies of efforts to upgrade moral reasoning in early childhood, an investigation by Kohlberg and a colleague illustrates the research being done with older children. They examined the reactions of several groups of students to their moral education technique: upper-middle-class 11- and 12-year-old Jewish students in a religion class; sixth and tenth grade lower-middle-class whites and middle-lower-class blacks; and students in a high school law course of mixed socio-economic and racial background. Some of the students in each of these groups were exposed to moral dilemmas, were made aware of different points of view, and were encouraged to argue and discuss each dilemma with students at adjacent stages of moral development. Other students in each group were exposed to lectures on the same material; still others spent their time on ordinary classroom activities. The investigators concluded that the much greater gain of the first group over the second two groups "...indicates an effect not due to time, re-testing, or participating in an experiment.... Still more important, the change which occurred was primarily genuine stimulation of development rather than the verbal learning of moral cliches" (Blatt and Kohlberg, 1975, pp.152-53). The change upward of approximately one full stage for the average member of the first group was seen to hold constant one year later.

On the basis of this and several other studies they review, the authors take the position that "If brief periods of classroom discussion can have a substantial effect on moral development, a pervasive, enduring and psychologically sound concern for the school's influence upon moral development should have much deeper and more positive effects" (Blatt and Kohlberg, 1975, p. 153).

A second conclusion these authors draw from comparing studies across pre-adolescent and adolescent age groups is that the period from age 10 to 14 is critical in moral development. Change is less likely in the two previous years. But this does not preclude the possibility of a similar critical period in the early childhood years. This writer believes that studies of other areas of development indicate the importance of both early childhood and adolescent periods. We may find that younger children need to deal more actively with problems more closely related to their daily lives. In line with this position, Sanborn suggests that:

> the main experiential determinants of moral development seem to be amount and variety of social experience, and the opportunity to take a number of roles and encounter other perspectives. Thus middle-class and popular children progress farther and faster than do lower-class children and social isolates (Sanborn, 1971, pp.148-49).

An approach to moral education which is specifically designed to promote seeing one's own experiences from the perspective of others is called "values clarification."

Raths, Harmin and Simon: Theory of Values

Values clarification is a less direct way than Kohlberg's of helping people achieve moral attitudes and beliefs about life. Rather than telling the individual what a principled position would be, it emphasizes personal discovery through wide-ranging discussions with others. The teacher never criticizes a student's position; the method assumes that discussion itself will produce more highly principled values. The technique attempts to clarify values not only in terms of moral dilemmas, but also toward a whole host of variables in life. It seems to work as well with young children as with adults.

This approach was initiated when the late research psychologist Louis Raths became convinced that unclear values, while a serious problem in their own right, were beginning to cause many related difficulties. Schools, he argued, have long been sensitive to the effects on learning of physical handicaps, emotional disturbance and, more recently, of "learning disabilities." These three deterents to productive learning are dealt with well in the schools today.

It has become apparent, however, that a fourth deterent to learning, lack of motivation, is frequently caused by personal confusion about values. People who are unclear about their values tend to be flighty, indecisive, apathetic, inconsistent, over-conforming or over-dissenting, and superficial role players. This has been an increasingly serious problem.

Values can be likened to guidelines which give direction to life. When the guidelines are blurred or unclear, people are conflicted and have difficulty making decisions. People who have clear values, on the other hand, tend to be positive, purposeful, and enthusiastic about life.

How does this confusion come about? In large measure, it happens because of the bombardment of ideas from television, radio, and print, as well as the exposure to enormous numbers of friends and acquaintances which urban society and modern communication make possible.

As Sidney Simon, a psychologist at the University of Massachusetts, has put it:

> The children and youth of today are confronted by many more choices than in previous generations...Modern society has made them less provincial and more sophisticated, but the complexity of these times has made the act of choosing infinitely more difficult (Simon *et al.*, 1972, p. 15).

More specifically, what is meant by the term "values"? Valuing, according to Raths, is composed of seven processes:

(1) *Prizing and cherishing.*   If a value is truly a value to us we have a sense of being glad about it. We are proud to be the kind of person who has such a value.

(2) *Publicly affirming, when appropriate.*   If we are really proud of a value we hold, we should be willing to let anyone else know that we feel that way.

(3) *Choosing from alternatives.*   A value which we hold because we have no choice but to hold it is no value at all. There must have been alternatives which we could have chosen, but decided not to.

(4) *Choosing after consideration of consequences.*   Obviously, a snap judgment about the importance of something does not really indicate a deep value. Only when we have given careful thought to the results of our decision can we be said to have a true value.

(5) *Choosing freely.*   If we are being forced by someone else to take a particular position, it cannot be said to really be our own value. As someone put it, "When we have to do something, we are not sure we want to, and we're pretty sure we don't."

(6) *Acting.*   Often we hear people say that they hold a particular value, but when called upon to do something about it, they are unwilling to act. A real value should be one on which we are willing to take action.

(7) *Acting with pattern, consistency, and repetition.*   In the case of a true value, we should be willing not only to act but to act as part of our normal pattern. People can see this is the way we really feel about a particular issue because this is the way we regularly act about it.

Clearly we should not expect these criteria to apply to the value systems of most young children. These seven characteristics serve mainly as a description of the fully formed value.

There are four basic ways that we acquire values:

(1) *Moralizing.*   This is the most direct way that adults have of in-

culcating their values in the young. It is traditionally the way we have taught children to believe what we think they should believe. It is harder and harder to use this method these days and it is becoming less effective. The direct inculcation of values really only works when everyone agrees which values are desirable. As was suggested earlier, this used to be the case in our country. It is no longer so. Today there are many different groups and individuals competing with each other to convince our young people what they should believe. This competition for the attention of young individuals is a major cause of values confusion.

(2) *A laissez-faire attitude.* Some people feel that we should just leave children alone and they will come to their own attitudes and values by themselves. A growing number of parents seem to have this attitude today. However, it, too, contributes to the many conflicts and confusions that young people are feeling.

(3) *Modeling.* In this case, we do not tell the young person what to think, but by presenting a good example, by being an attractive model, we hope that they will come to imitate us. As with moralizing, however, the problem is that there are so many models for children to imitate. Modern communications techniques have increased the number of models a hundredfold. This method, therefore, doesn't seem to work very well either.

(4) *Values clarification.* As Simon describes it:

> ...Thus, the values clarification approach does not aim to instill any particular set of values. The goals of the values clarification approach is to help students utilize the above seven processes of valuing in their own lives; to apply these value processes to already formed behavior patterns, and to those still emerging (Simon, *et al.,* 1972, p. 20).

> ...The values clarification approach tries to help young people answer some of these questions and build their own value system. It is not a new approach. There have always been parents, teachers, and other educators who have sought ways to help young people think through values issues for themselves. They have done this in many ways (Simon, *et al.,* 1972, pp. 18-19).

Many techniques for helping youngsters make decisions about their own value structure have been designed in the last decade. Simon, *et al.,* (1972) and Howe and Howe (1975) have suggested over 100 specific and highly practical strategies which help school-aged children build the values process into their lives. Several of these strategies will now be described, followed by strategies appropriate for pre-schoolers.

Values Clarification Strategies

(1) *Values voting.*   The teacher reads questions to the class and asks "How many of you...(wish you were an only child?)" Those who do raise their hands, those who don't point thumbs down, and those undecided fold their arms. The teacher puts the vote for each question on the board. When the voting is completed, discussion starts. Some sample questions are:

How many of you:

(a)   Think black people are as nice as whites?
(b)   Would rather live someplace else?
(c)   Like school?
(d)   Get enough sleep at night?
(e)   Have a best friend?
(f)   Like to be teased?
(g)   Are afraid of the dark?
(h)   Think it's all right for boys to play with dolls?

(2) *Forced Choice Ladder.*   The children construct a ladder with three to eight steps.

FIGURE 6.

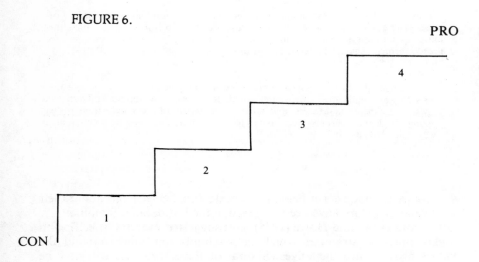

The teacher suggests several ideas, objects, happenings, facts, names, etc. (make a ladder with the same number of steps). Each child then writes his favorite on the top, and so on. For example, four holidays could be suggested. When everyone has completed the task, one child at a time tells his choices and why. Ideas are compared.

Some examples are:

      (a)   Doctor, lawyer, garbage man, salesman.
      (b)   Liar, cheater, bully, borrower.
      (c)   Mother, father, brother, sister.

(3) *Value Whips.*   This is a means by which children and teachers can see how others react to various issues. Someone poses a question to the class, then after a few minutes thinking time, "whips" around the room asking students to give their answers. Sample questions are:

      (a)   What is something you're proud of?
      (b)   What is a choice you made today?
      (c)   What is a favorite thing to do?
      (d)   What is something you're afraid of?

(4) *I Wonder Statements.*   This method is designed to stimulate probing, critical attitudes. After doing some other values clarification exercise, the teacher asks the students to complete such sentences as these:

      (a)   I wonder if...
      (b)   I wonder about...
      (c)   I wonder why...
      (d)   I wonder when...

(5) *Brainstorming.*   The idea here is to have the class generate as many imaginative reactions to a situation (attitudes, problem solutions, etc.) as possible. Students are encouraged to respond quickly, avoiding criticism of their own ideas or those of the others. Quantity is encouraged, as it eventually breeds quality. Humorous and even silly ideas are also encouraged; even if such ideas are not useful, they often spark ones that are. Try to get everyone to contribute; timid students frequently have excellent ideas. Some questions might be:

      (a)   How can we make this class a happier place to be?
      (b)   What would be an interesting topic for discussion?
      (c)   Who are the finest people you know?
      (d)   What is the best thing to do when you're bored? Scared?

(6) *Three Characters.*   Designed to help the child become clearer about his own goals, this approach asks "If you could be someone else,

which three people would you be?'' After each child has chosen, the teacher asks "Were your characters males or females?" "Would you be on anyone else's list?" "Would your best friend be able to guess who you put on your list?"

(7) *Magic Box.*   The teacher asks, "If you came home from school and found a magic box, what would you hope would be in it?"

(8) *Unfinished Sentences.*   Students are asked to complete unfinished sentences; this activity is aimed at revealing value indicators. For example:

      (a)   If I had my own car, I would...
      (b)   I like it best when people...
      (c)   If I had a thousand dollars...
      (d)   Secretly I wish...
      (e)   It makes me cry when...

(9) *Who Comes to Your House?*   The children list all the people they can remember who have come to their house during the past year. Next to the list of names, they make six columns. In Column One, they put an *R* if the person is a relative, an *F* if he is a friend, and an *O* for others. In Column Two, they put an *M* if the person's manners bother them. In Column Three, they place a star next to the names of the persons they were really glad to see. In Column Four, they put an *X* next to names of persons they would rather never came back. In Column Five, they put an *S* or a *D* if the person's religion is the same or different from theirs. In Column Six, they put an *SR* or *DR* if the person's race is the same or different from theirs. The typical response in each column is looked at and discussed.

(10) *The "What Is Important" Song.*   The teacher plays the song "What Is Important" on the guitar or the piano (see p. 326 of *Values Clarification,* Simon, *et al.*); when the line "Tell me if you know" is reached, any child who wants to fills in his idea.

(11) *Baker's Dozen.*   The teacher says "Make a list of 13 things you use around your house that run on electricity. If you can't think of 13, make a list of as many as you can. Draw a line through the things you don't really need. Now draw a circle around the three things you'd be lost without." A discussion, as usual, follows.

(12) *The Suitcase.*   Pretending that the class is going to take a long trip, the teacher asks the students to list what they would pack in one large suitcase. To vary the situation, the teacher can describe what the land to which the class is traveling is like—agricultural and very poor, an oasis, etc.

Whereas a large variety of values clarification techniques exist for school-aged children, practically no strategies have yet been designed for preschoolers. It seems clear, however, that the major goal for 3- and 4-year-olds should be to improve the ability to make a simple choice. The following activities should be carried out in small discussion groups. The parent or teacher should encourage each child to explain his choice as much as possible.

(1) *Which Is Better?* In this game, two choices are offered and the child must choose one as better than the other. If possible, a picture of each choice in the pair (e.g., cut from a magazine) is first held up for all to see. Of course, the actual objects are best.

(a) *Tastes*
Ice cream or spinach?
Stones or jelly beans?
Mashed potatoes or french fries?
Pickles or carrots?

(b) *Touch Sensations*
Bunny fur or bricks?
Mommy's hand or Grandma's hand?
Mud or snow?
Warm sudsy water or icy cold water?

(c) *Sounds*
Crying or laughing?
Singing or yelling?
Truck horns or police sirens?
A motorcycle or roller skates?

(d) *Smells*
Cookies or soap?
Mommy or Daddy?
Rain or snow?
Coffee or coke?

(e) *General*
Clean or dirty?
Short or tall?
Hot or cold?
When using the toilet, standing up or sitting down?
Biting or kissing?

(2) *Who Can Tell What I'm Thinking of?* This is played the same way as the above example.

(a) Things that are nice to take to bed with us.

(b) Things that make us scared (happy, sad, angry, proud, etc.).
(c) Clothing that is hard to put on (easy).
(d) The best part of a "busy box."
(e) The best animal in the world.
(f) Favorite toys.
(g) Things that are easy to lose and hard to find?
(h) Favorite relative.
(i) Things that hurt people's feelings (cheer them up, etc.).

Although only two examples of strategy are given here, it seems to me that others would have to be quite similar to these two. A large variety of value objects (eg., things that hurt people's feelings) can be readily imagined. They should be chosen on the basis of relevancy to the interests and experience of the children being dealt with.

Several new books on strategies for values clarification are listed in the bibliography with asterisks next to the author's name. Together they present a wealth of ideas for these on-going activities.

The major criticism that has been made of values clarification has been of its central tenet: whereas teachers must never evaluate the values expressed by the students, nevertheless some students occasionally espouse "unacceptable" values. Certainly it does happen that a student says he favors a value with which almost no one else in our society would agree. Simor argues strongly, however, that teachers must allow such value statements to stand, relying on group pressure to change that student's mind. Another criticism is that most teachers will use subtle means to condition the values they want chosen. Experience seems to indicate, however, that teachers do this anyway, and that values clarification training makes them less likely to do it.

Conclusions

After a long hiatus, moral education is recovering its once important role in American schools. This is due in part to a growing concern among educators and parents for the ethical values (or lack of them) in today's society. It is also partly due to the innovative research of several psychologists.

This research has led to two major theories of moral development. Piaget suggests that there are four stages of the practice of moral behavior, and three stages of understanding. Each is closely governed by the unfolding of mental processes, and proceeds on a schedule with each stage covering several years. Kohlberg describes six levels of morality, which are also developmental. He believes that this development is governed far more by experience than does Piaget, however. He finds that the majority of adults never progress beyond the middle two levels, and argues that only with appropriate education will they be likely to reach the highest levels.

Kohlberg's approach to moral education is quite directive. He poses moral dilemmas to students, and then attempts to raise each person's morality by exposing him to resolutions one level above his current level. Simon and his associates have taken a more non-directive approach. This technique, called "values clarification," relies on the discussion of moral dilemmas by a group to expose the irrationality of unethical opinions in the group. Over 100 strategies for clarifying values have been designed.

REFERENCES

Beck, C.M., Crittenden, B.S., and Sullivan, E.V. *Moral Education,* New York: Newman Press, 1971.*

Bee, Helen. *The Developing Child,* New York: Harper and Row, 1975.

Hartshorne, H. and May, M.S. *Studies in the Nature of Character,* (3 vols.), New York: Macmillan, 1928-1930.

Hoffman, M.L. "Moral Development." P.H. Mussen (Ed). *Carmichael's Manual of Child Psychology.* (3rd Ed.), Vol. 2, New York: Wiley, 1970.

Howe, L. and Howe, M. *Personalizing Education,* New York: Hart, 1975.*

Kohlberg, L. "The Development of Children's Orientation Toward a Moral Order: I. Sequence in the Development of Moral Thought." *Vita Humana,* 1963, 6, pp.11-33.

____. "Development of Moral Character and Moral Ideology." M.L. Hoffman and L.W. Hoffman (Eds.). *Review of Child Development Research,* Vol. 1, New York: Russell Sage Foundation, 1964.

____. "Moral Development and Identification." H.W. Stevenson (Ed.). *Child Psychology: 62nd Yearbook of the National Society for the Study of Education.* Chicago: University of Chicago Press, 1963.

____. "Moral Education in the Schools: A Developmental View." *School Review,* 74, 1966, pp. 1-30.

____. "Moral Education, Religious Education, and the Public Schools: A Developmental View." T. Sizer (Ed.). *Religion and Public Education,* Boston: Houghton Mifflin, 1967.

Kohlberg, L. and Turiel, E. *Research in Moral Development: The Cognitive Developmental Approach.* New York: Holt, Rinehart and Winston, 1971.*

Milgram S. "Behaviorial Study of Obedience." *Journal of Abnormal Social Psychology,* 1963, 67, pp. 371-378.

____. "Some Conditions of Obedience and Disobedience to Authority." *Human Relations,* 1965, 18, pp. 67-76.

Piaget, J. *The Moral Judgement of the Child,* New York: Collier, 1962.

Raths, L., Merrill, H., and Simon, S. *Values and Teaching,* Columbus, Ohio: Merrill, 1966.

Sears, R.R., Rau, L. and Alpert, R. *Identification and Child Rearing.* Stanford: Stanford University Press, 1965.

Simon S.B., Howe, L.W., and Kirschenbaum, H. *Values Clarification,* New York: Hart 1972.*

Sverdlova, O. (Ed.). *Ot Nolya Do Semi (From Zero to Seven),* Moscow: Znanic Publishers, 1967.

Turiel, Elliot. "An Experimental Test of the Sequentiality of Developmental Stages in the Child's Moral Judgments." *Journal of Personality and Social Psychology,* 1966, 3, pp. 611-618.

*Especially good for exercises.

VIII.

THE EFFECT OF TELEVISION: A Look by Pre-schoolers

By Brian Brightly

In 1972 the Office of the Surgeon General of the United States released a report on television's use and effects. The report has serious implications for America's viewing, especially as it relates to "the new children." It contains valuable data about viewing habits, influence on behavior, and the relationship between television violence and aggressive behavior. While the results of the study were scientifically and cautiously stated, the Surgeon General, Jesse Steinfeld, commented that the relationship between television violence and antisocial behavior is sufficient to warrant appropriate remedial action.

The Surgeon General's report and the reaction to it dramatize television's enormous impact on our lives and the need to inform parents and teachers about its potential effect upon children. To analyze its influence, we need to know some characteristics of the 2-6-year-old child and then determine how television acts as a teacher for these children. Some guidelines for parents and teachers should emerge from the discussion.

The Children

The Surgeon General's report offers some interesting and valuable information about the viewing habits of children. It reported that television has become a major subject of children's conversation, with about one half saying they have been frightened by what they had seen. Children who watch frequently tend to dream about television shows, while those who watch least are more likely to be frightened by it. More than half of the children surveyed studied while watching television. A favorite form of punishment is to deprive children of television viewing, or permitting more television as a reward. One interesting finding has been that the more passive child tends to heavy viewing. This finding is particularly pertinent when we consider the discussion of early experience and intelligence: a child requires *active* involvement with the environment for adequate learning and mental development. But before we begin a more detailed examination of television's role as a teacher, it is well to reflect upon some growth characteristics of the 2- 6-year-old child.

One characteristic that should concern us is the child's rapid growth from 2 to 6 years. Height increases from 2 feet to almost 4 feet; weight from 27 pounds to about 48 pounds; and perhaps most importantly, a child's vocabulary grows from about 50-100 words at age 2, to about 3000 words at age 6. This is a conservative estimate of vocabulary development for these years, but it emphasizes the necessity for a stimulating linguistic environment that will prepare the youngster for reading.

Television, properly used, can be a positive influence during these years, but we must have a clear and honest understanding of pros and cons. Only then can we use television to facilitate both physical and mental development.

Television: The Teacher

It is time to put the pre-shooler in front of a television set. Many of our teachers have been the models that have shaped and influenced our lives. In the early grades great importance is placed on the teacher role.

In fact, the "teacher is the curriculum." A new teacher is now very much in evidence—one who is only 25 years old. What is this teacher teaching? Does he deserve tenure?

Thomas Hutchinson wrote a book in 1946 called *Here is Television: Your Window to the World.* In this book he describes his perspective of what television would do.

> Television means the world in your home, and in the homes of all the people of the world. It is the greatest means of communication ever developed by the mind of man. It should do more to develop friendly neighbors, and to bring understanding and peace on earth, than any other single material force in the world today.

Television is in over 95 percent of all American homes, according to the Television Information Office in New York, but the dream of developing friends and bringing peace is still unrealized.

Evelyn Kaye in her book *The Family Guide to Children's Television* presents a good summary of the diet being fed pre-schoolers on Saturday network programs. Kaye points out that there is little examination of the implications of the story lines of these cartoons, particularly with regard to testing or research. Animation companies such as Hanna-Barbera are not expected to conduct any research on the content of the program. (See Figure 7.)

George Comstock provides further data that describes the extent to which children are exposed to this teacher, "the television." He cites research showing that children begin viewing television regularly between 3 and 4 years prior to entering first grade. In addition, most children watch television every day for two hours or more.

In one study by J. P. Murray on inner-city homes, it was found that kindergarten and first grade children's viewing ranged from 5 to 42 hours per week. Comstock also observes that the viewing increases during elementary school years, peaks at sixth grade, then decreases during the high school period. The best average, after examining all of the data on pre-school viewing, ranges from 15 to 26 hours per week, at least as many instructional hours as a teacher spends in the classroom. So the television as a teacher is getting the exposure.

Dorothy Cohen points out a study at Michigan State that reveals interesting statistics with regard to exposure for pre-schoolers. The survey done in 1971 showed 490,000 toddlers watching "Mannix" and another 453,000 watching "Hawaii Five-O," both shown at 10:00 p.m. At an earlier hour, more than 1 million 2- to 5-year-olds viewed "Adam-12," the "FBI," "Gunsmoke," "High Chapparal," "Men of Shiloh," "Mod Squad," and "Mission Impossible."

It appears that television as a teacher already has tenure by default. Young children are exposed to these models, but what about the content? The evidence to date suggests the following contentions:

Television, the teacher, affects the beliefs and the behavior of young persons.

FIGURE 7. SATURDAY MORNING NETWORK PROGRAMS
1974-1975 SCHEDULE

	ABC	CBS	NBC
8:00	Yogi and His Friends*	Speed Buggy*	Adams Family*
8:30	Bugs Bunny*	Scooby Doo, Where Are You?*	Chopper Bunch*
9:00	Kung Phooey*	Jeannie*	Emergency + 4*
9:30	The New Adventures of Gilligan*	Partridge Family: 2200 A.D.* In the News (8 2-minute segments on hour and half-hour from 8 to noon)	Run, Joe, Run*
10:00	Devlin*	Valley of the Dinosaurs*	Land of the Lost*
10:30	Krog: 70,000 B.C.*	Shazam!*	Sigmund and the Sea Monsters
11:00		Harlem Globetrotters Popcorn Machine*	The Pink Panther Show*
11:30	Super Friends*	Hudson Bros. Razzle Dazzle Comedy Show	Star Trek*
12:00	These Are the Days	U.S. of Archie*	Jetsons*
12:30		Fat Albert and the Cosby Kids*	GO!
1:00	American Bandstand		
1:30		CBS Children's Film Festival	

*Animated Cartoon

Television violence has influenced young persons toward aggression and anti-social behavior.

Television has created a "consumption environment" for young persons.

The Televised Society

In supporting the first contention, Aimee Dorr Leifer speaks about television as a provider of a social system for children. Most of the social information on televison is found in entertainment programming, and Leifer describes this social system. A summary of her evidence would emphasize the frequencies of violence in the social system. Characteristic of this violence is that it is often unaccompanied by emotions other than humor and that it occurs in situations counter to the norms of most adults in society. Women and minority groups are also under-represented and often portrayed as incompetent and one-dimensional.

Television and Sex Identity

Television, the teacher, offers symbolic lessons to its students, the children—symbolic lessons about sex identity, race, occupations, and the meaning of violence. All of these models portray a world view to the child.

George Gerbner, dean of the University of Pennsylvania's Annenberg School of Communications, is quoted in *The Early Window:*

> Representation in the fictional world (of television) signifies social existence; absence means symbolic annihilation. Being buffeted by events and victimized by people denotes social impotence; ability to wrest events about, to act freely, boldly, and effectively, is a mark of dramatic importance and social power. Values and forces come to play through characterizations; good is a certain type of attractiveness, evil is a personality defect, and right is the might that wins...The issue is rarely in doubt, the action is typically a game of personality, group identification, skill, and power...Symbolic hurt to symbolic people and causes can show real people how they might use or avoid to stay alive and advance their causes...

Gerbner's study indicates that sex identity is most powerful with the white, young married middle-class American male. He represents fully half of all leading television characters. He is likely to be involved in violence as an aggressor and is less likely than other characters to be punished for his aggression. Women, on the other hand, make up only one quarter of all television characters. Two of every three women are married. They are less successful when they are involved in aggression and usually appear in a sexual, romantic or family role. Married women are less likely to be victims than single women and employed women are villains more often than housewives. Women are also depicted as less law-abiding than men.

Sex role inequity is even found in some of the best educational programs. Rita Dohrmann from Drake University conducted a sex-role analysis in 1974 of "Sesame Street," "Electric Company," "Misterogers' Neighborhood," and "Captain Kangeroo." "The least recognized age/sex status on programs designed for children's edification is that of half their viewing audience, the female child." Dohrmann cites 100 percent male central characters. The female role models most often exhibit patterns of following rather than leading, praising instead of being rewarded, and are seen as fearful seekers of protection rather than self-determined individuals. The most sensitive indicator of the difference in value allocation to the sexes in this study is that of bravery-reserve/helplessness. Dohrmann states that males, being self-possessed and responsible for others, meet the world as subjects, whereas females, lacking self-confidence, face the world as objects. "Tom Terrific in 'Captain Kangaroo,' Super Grover of 'Sesame Street,' and Letterman of 'Electric Company,' freely roam the universe to save some element of it from disaster. Women shriek when in haunted houses, are rescued from mashers by burly boyfriends, and continually ask directions."

These kinds of gender problems continue to plague some of the highest quality educational programming. In fairness to Children's Television Workshop, a great deal of research has continued in this area of sex and role identification. The newer productions of "Sesame Street" and "Electric Company" depict a much greater sensitivity to these issues.

Television and Stereotypes

Additional research presents some interesting studies on ethnic stereotypes and occupational roles. Misconceptions of ethnic groups have not improved appreciably over the last 15 years. In an early study, Italians were law-breakers over half the time they were presented. Present studies still conclude that foreigners as a group were more likely to become involved in violence and get punished for it than were the Americans.

The status of blacks has changed considerably. Cedric Clark, a black psychologist at Stanford University speaks of the components of recognition and respect. Blacks have recognition, but the respect in a variety of role models on television depends upon one's perspective. Clark refers to the present black images as "regulators." These are defined as supportors of the status quo in society.

George Gerbner in *The Early Window* provides an excellent summary of the occupational roles played out in television programs. The summary has particular relevance to the present educational emphasis on career education at both national and state levels. In the early sixties only six of ten television characters had jobs, and they were usually middle or upper class. Blue collar workers represented less than one tenth of the characters and were usually presented in a negative light. Gerbner quotes Defleur's summary of the model cues presented by television in occupational roles:

> Among both males and females, professional workers were substantially over-represented. Nearly a third of the labor force on television was engaged in professional occupations of relatively high social prestige. A similar concentration was noted in the category of managers, officials, and proprietors. This bias in the direction of the higher socio-economic strata is especially sharp for males...while nearly half the males in the actual labor force...held jobs in commerce and industry as operatives, craftsmen, and related workers, less than a tenth did so on television...Thus, on the programs sampled there were more deep-sea divers than factory workers, more helicopter pilots than supermarket clerks, more night-club singers than salesgirls.

Television as a teacher of social behavior has so far failed to live up to Thomas Hutchinson's ideals. The extended discussion in this area is meant to emphasize the continued exposure of these role models throughout childhood, day after day, week after week. There is no data to assume that a child is converted to another value system of role models than that which he sees on television. On the contrary, television as a teacher provides an environment that becomes real to the pre-schooler.

Violence and Aggression

Consumers of television have been greatly concerned with television violence and its relation to anti-social behavior. Gerbner states that:

> Young children are apparently learning from television that aggression is a good strategy, or at least an exceedingly common one. They are not learning the contextual message that crime doesn't pay or that alternatives to aggression are desirable. When children are given a mixed message about the context for aggression on television, they come away believing simply that the more aggression they see, the more they should aggress. This is especially true for young children.

Television, as the teacher of violence and aggression, is substantiated by Gerbner's studies on the amount of violence appearing during the period of 1967-1972. Gerbner and his colleagues observed in October of each year the amount of violence portrayed in a one week schedule. He separated the program material into plays or skits. In 1969 eight of ten plays contained violence, with five violent episodes per play. The most violent programs were cartoons that were specifically designed for children. He reported that the average cartoon in 1967 contained three times as many violent episodes as the average adult dramatic hour. In 1969 there was a violent episode at least every two minutes on Saturday mornings. The average cartoon had nearly 12 times the violence rate of the average movie hour. Gerbner's study shows that during this five year period violence on television did not decrease at any appreciable rate.

The real issue is not whether violence is portrayed by this "teacher", the television set, but what its effect is on children. We must go beyond the limp conclusions provided by the Surgeon Genral's report. Aimee Leifer and Donald Roberts performed a study on aggression based on a response hierachy. They used a sample of 271 youngsters from kindergarten to the 12th grade, showing such programs as "Batman", "Adam-12" and "Rifleman." This laboratory test concluded that "whatever analysis was performed, the amount of violence in the program affected the amount of aggression subsequently chosen." Stein and Friedrich observed 97 pre-school children in a field study of the effects of aggressive and prosocial television. They attempted to control socio-economic status, intelligence and amounts of home viewing. The aggressive programs were "Batman" and "Superman," and the prosocial programs were episodes of "Misterogers' Neighborhood." The most important measure was the observations of the children during free play or in the classroom. The results of the study showed that children who viewed aggressive programming were more likely to be aggressive in interpersonal situations than children who viewed prosocial television. The editors of the five compliations of research done in *The Early Window* summarize their findings on aggression by pointing out the great degree of convergence on all the evidence that exposure to television violence can, and often does, cause viewers to be significantly more aggressive.

George Comstock presents a poll of researchers on the issue of violence and aggression in television. One can select the researcher of his choice and formulate an hypothesis. The difficulty in coming up with definitive answers is that one can no longer study the effect of television apart from the child's environment. One cannot study effects only in a laboratory, since researchers have not really had that much time to determine the full effect of this conveyor of information. A researcher included in Comstock's poll, R. E. Goranson, stated that:

> Novel, aggressive behavior sequences are learned by children through exposure to realistic portrayals of aggression on television or in films...The actual performance of aggressive behaviors learned from the media is largely contingent on the child's belief in the effectiveness of aggression in attaining his goals...The mass media typically present aggression as a highly effective form of behavior.

Sooner or later the reader must follow Evelyn Kaye's suggestion: Sit down and take a dose of pre-school television programming. What do you see in the program activity? What is your opinion of how a child's behavior might be affected?

The Consumption Environment

One could not write about the effect of television on children without referring to the foundation upon which the program activity is built—namely, commercials. My 4-year-old daughter recently presented me with her Christmas list. She wants in this order:

(1) Putt-Putt Speedway
(2) Barbie Doll and Barbie Townhouse
(3) Super Heroes Dolls and Trucks
(4) Barbie Beauty Center
(5) Batman and Robin Dolls
(6) Walking Baby I Love You
(7) Hoppity House
(8) Weebles Buried Treasure

Television sells, and advertisers sponsor over 6 billion dollars worth of television time. According to Dan Bagdikian, the keynote speaker at the 1975 NAEB Conference, the average television set really costs an additional $95.00 because the consumer pays for the inflationary prices of the products. The sponsors merely pass on their advertising costs to the consumer. So, we pay from the wallet and we also pay by having to live with commercials.

There has been a major movement over the years to remove the commercial world away from children. Action For Children's Television is one major group that has petitioned the FCC and others to reduce and eventually remove commercials from children's programming. The rationale for such a request is based primarily on the misuse of persuasive selling tactics on young, indiscriminate children. There are other issues which deal with the actual products themselves. The majority of products have little nutritional or redemptive value. (See Figure 8.)

Sustaining the consumption environment continues to be a major objective of television. Studies shown by Liebert, Neale and Davidson suggest a great attention to commercials at age 5 and decreasing attention to age 11. The kindergarten child often did not discriminate between advertisement and product advertised. The majority of the 9-12-year olds were suspicious of the commercials and believed them to be untrue. Additional research on the effect of commercials on younger children is being collected and investigated under the direction of Dr. Gerald Lesser at Harvard. Examination of this kind should provide additional evidence for research needed to substantiate dissolution of commercials for young children.

The sponsors have ultimately been the prime movers in changing the commercials, due to public opinion. The removal of vitamin ads from children's programming by the drug companies was one such event. Ac-

FIGURE 8. JUNE 19, 1971: 8:00 A.M. TO 9:30 A.M.

BUGS BUNNY/ROADRUNNER HOUR

			Minutes
8:00:00	PM	"Bugs Bunny/Roadrunner Hour" (Intro.)	1.75
8:01:45	CA	(Kool Aid)	.50
8:02:15	CA	(Kool Pop)	.50
8:02:45	PM	"Bunker Hill Bunny" (Cartoon)	6.67
8:09:25	CA	(Romper Room's Inchworm Toy)	.50
8:09:55	CA	(Grape Tang)	.50
8:10:25	PM	(Roadrunner Song and Chase) (Transition)	.42
8:10:50	CA	(General Mill's Count Chocula Cereal)	.50
8:11:20	CA	(General Mill's Cheerio's)	.50
8:11:50	PM	"Tweety's Circus" (Cartoon)	6.57
8:18:25	CA	(Keebler's Cookies)	.50
8:18:55	CA	(Keebler's Cookies)	.50
8:19:25	PM	"Bugs Bunny/Roadrunner Hour" (Transition)	.42
8:19:50	CA	(Mattel's Dawn Doll)	.50
8:20:20	CA	(Mattel's Zoomer Boomer)	.50
8:20:50	PM	"Gee Whizz" (Cartoon)	5.83
8:26:40	CA	(Post Sugar Crisp)	.50
8:27:10	CA	(Kool Pop)	.50
8:27:40	PM	"Stay tuned for part two" (Transition)	.42
8:28:05	NCA	"Keep Boston Clean"	.17
8:28:15	CA	(Birdseye Libbyland Frozen Dinners)	1.00
8:29:15	ID	"WHDH-TV" (VO): "Lassie" as visual	.08
8:29:20	PM	"Bugs Bunny/Roadrunner Hour" (Transition)	.50
8:29:50	CA	(Kellogg's Raisin Bran)	.50
8:30:20	PM	"Hare Ways to the Stars" (Cartoon)	6.25
8:36:35	CA	(Nestle's Quik)	.50
8:37:05	CA	(Nestle's $100,000 Bar)	.50
8:37:35	PM	"Bugs Bunny/Roadrunner Hour" (Transition)	.50
8:38:05	CA	(General Mill's Cheerio's)	.50
8:38:35	CA	(Kenner's SST Racer)	.50
8:39:05	PM	"Highway Runnery" (Cartoon)	6.00
8:45:05	CA	(Hershey Bars)	.50
8:45:35	CA	(Old Spice for Father's Day)	.50
8:46:05	PM	"Bugs Bunny/Roadrunner Hour" (Transition)	.50
8:46:35	CA	(General Mill's Count Chocula/Frankenberry)	1.00
8:47:35	PM	"Bonanza Bunny" (Cartoon)	5.84
8:53:25	CA	(Quaker Cereals—Willy Wonka premium)	1.00
8:54:25	Promo	"Groovie Ghoulies and Sabrina"	.33
8:54:45	PM	"Bugs Bunny/Roadrunner Hour" (Visuals, Credits)	1.08
8:55:50	NCA	(Seat Belts)	.33

IN THE KNOW

			Minutes
8:56:10	PM	"In the Know"—"by Kellogg's"	.33
8:56:30	CA	(Kellogg's Rice Krispies)	.50
8:57:00	PM	"In the Know"—"Saturday in Rome"	1.68
8:58:40	Promo	(Captain Kangaroo) (CBS)	.33
8:59:00	CA	(McDonald's)	.50
8:59:30	NCA	(Boy's Club of America)	.50

THE GROOVIE GHOULIES AND
SABRINA THE TEENAGE WITCH

			Minutes
9:00:00	ID	"WHDH-TV Boston" (Identification)	.08
9:00:05	PM	"Groovie Ghoulies…" (Jokes a la Laugh-In)	2.42
9:02:30	PM	"Hansel and Gretel" (Cartoon)	2.67
9:05:10	PM	"Horrible Horrorscope" (Cartoon)	2.08
9:07:15	CA	(General Mill's Count Chocula Cereal)	.50
9:07:45	CA	(Tang)	.50
9:08:15	PM	"Don't go away" (Transition)	.50
9:08:45	CA	(Romper Room's Inchworm Toy)	.50
9:09:15	CA	(General Mill's Count Chocula/Frankenberry)	.50
9:09:45	PM	"Beach Party" (Cartoon)	3.58
9:13:20	CA	(Pillsbury's Funny Face)	.50
9:13:50	CA	(Stuckey's—"Happy Highways" premium)	.50
9:14:20	PM	"Stick around" (Transition)	.33
9:14:40	CA	(Kellogg's Special K)	.50
9:15:10	CA	(Kellogg's Frosted Mini-Wheat)	.50
9:15:40	PM	"Beach Party" (Continued)	5.42
9:21:05	PM	"Don't go away" (Transition)	.33
9:21:25	CA	(Mattel's Dawn Doll and Friends)	.50
9:21:55	CA	(Shasta Soda)	.25
9:22:10	CA	(Burger King)	.50
9:22:40	PM	"Noises are the Strangest Things in the World" (Song)	2.67
9:25:20	CA	(Quaker Cereal's—Willy Wonka premium)	1.00
9:26:20	PM	"Don't go away" (Transition)	.58
9:26:55	Promo	"The Week Ends Here"	.25
9:27:10	CA	(Spokies)	.50
9:27:40	CA	(McDonald's)	.50
9:28:10	ID	"WHDH-TV Boston" (Visual Red Sox)	.09
9:28:15	PM	"Stick around" (Transition)	.42
9:28:40	CA	(Sizzler's Fat Track)	.50
9:29:15	PM	"Weird Window Time" (Jokes a la Laugh-In)	3.34

tion For Children's Television generated enough public opinion to act as the catalyst in that major move in 1972.

Television is still teaching consumption, and most parents have to cope with Christmas lists that were completed without their input or influence. There is hope for the future. Part of that hope is reflected in the third category.

Television: Responding to the Needs of Children

During the last three years I have asked school administrators across the country, "what muppet lives in a garbage can?" Only one third of my audience knew the answer. I have not met any group of 3- or 4-year-olds who do not know where Oscar lives! "Sesame Street" exploded on the television scene with the impact of an intellectual firecracker. The coming of Sesame Street made two things clear: television, used properly, could become the modern age's most powerful and effective purveyor of information, and learning could be fun!

Prior to the success of "Sesame Street," instructional television was in trouble. The promises made to schools about all the things television would do were not being fulfilled. The majority of programming was low-cost and locally produced. Most programming was teacher-centered and produced in sterile studio environments. Programs were neither good production nor good teaching. Schools were discouraged. They had spent many federal and state dollars for equipment. High program quality was simply not available.

"Sesame Street" rekindled a rapidly dying flame, to the extent that it provided a model for educators to follow. Gerald Lesser's book *Children and Television* gives an accounting of that model. The program's success can be attributed to a healthy blend of planning research and evaluation with high quality production capability. This model converted many who believed that television had lost its capacity for instruction. "Electric Company" was a second major series that achieved success. It substantially followed the "Sesame Street" developmental model. The research and feedback from both program activities indicate success. Viewers of the programs were better prepared for entrance into school.

There is also more recent evidence that "Sesame Street" contributes positively to the socialization process. Norman Felsenthal has described the environment that Children's Television Workshop has created with the characters in a variety of prosocial activities.

Since the Children's Television Workshop model, production quality has increased in instructional programming. Standards for research design, production and evaluation have been raised to a high level. Stations, states and private enterprise have been forced to reassess their program production acitivity. The model was established. Gerald Lesser had talked first about the needs and characteristics of children. Goals were then established, and the visual insights of the television production team were blended with the content specialists. Research, planning and more research, as well as human patience were keys to the success of these program materials. The process was important. Unlike the commercial world, the end did not justify the means. One simply couldn't achieve a quality product unless the process was carefully implemented.

Television: The Future Prospects

We have seen that the television medium possesses a potential for enrichment, as well as for great harm. Realizing the former and eliminating the latter are among the most essential challenges facing prospective parents and teachers.

There are at least two useful approaches to the curtailment of violent programs. First of all, let the networks, and particularly the sponsors know how you feel about certain programs and programming trends. Concerted and consistent pressure on those groups will eventually effect change. And second, we simply need to know more about how young children are affected by television and violent programs specifically. Eli Rubinstein, from the State University of New York at Stony Brook, states that:

> the age group about which we have the least information is the pre-school child. In the total sample of subjects in all of the studies undertaken in the Surgeon General's research program, only about 1 percent were under age 5 and none were under 3. Another 1 percent were of kindergarten age.

Logical decision making depends on knowledge. If we can support objections to certain kinds of programs with substantial research data, our efforts toward altering those programs will be greatly assisted.

While it may not be possible to immediately alter the nature of programming, it has already been shown that public opinion can have a powerful effect on commercials. Action for Children's Television, representing many thousands of concerned parents, was able to remove vitamin ads from children's programs. Continued vigilance will be needed to discern other forms of propaganda. Children need not be active members of the consumption environment.

Alternatives to commercial television programming are available to most sections of the country, and by the end of the decade will offer a rich variety of educational and entertainment options. Public television, in partnership with the educational community, is one such option. Recently we have seen programs of the highest educational and prosocial value. "Villa Allegre" and "Carrascollendas" are two series which teach linguistics, math and social concepts to children with bi-lingual and bi-cultural backgrounds. The "Zoom" series for pre-adolescents has contributed much to that community of children.

More recently state educational agencies have taken initiatives through a national cooperative called the Agency for Instructional Television. Program series in mental health, value education, life coping and career skills have most recently had impact upon students and teachers who use these media resources as learning tools in the classroom.

Public television has made great strides in providing adult programming in science, the arts and history. The Nova series in science, "Masterpiece Theatre" and the most recent history series "The Adams Chronicles" are all excellent examples of the prosocial power of this medium being used for adults.

Children will receive comparable programming through more intensive program efforts involving both education and the broadcasters. A recent report to the Corporation for Public Broadcasting from the Advisory Council of National Organizations submitted a list of priorities, the first of which would "Intensify efforts to bridge the traditional chasm between broadcasting and education, building a working partnership to serve their common purposes."

If this indeed happens, I predict our children will receive the inheritance that television has not yet fulfilled. A closer bond will move the broadcaster, both public and commercial, into a more sensitive awareness of the cognitive and affective learning needs of young children. A more comprehensive approach to research and assessment of children's needs by the educator, as well as greater fiscal commitment by the educational and broadcasting communities can and will result in a new role in television for children.

Further technological options are iminent. Alvin Toffler in *Future Shock,* described the prospects for television diversification:

> When technical breakthroughs alter the economics of television by providing more channels and lowering costs of production, we can anticipate that that medium too, will begin to fragment its output and cater to, rather than counter, the increasing diversity of the consuming public...The invention of electronic video recording, the spread of cable television, the possibility of broadcasting direct from satellite to cable systems, all point to vast increases in program variety (Toffler, 1974, p.281).

Rather than waste valuable time and resources on altering the nature of contemporary commercial programming, we should, instead, concentrate our efforts on realizing the full potential of the options before us. Plato in *The Republic* wrote:

> And shall we just carelessly allow children to hear any casual tales which may be devised by casual persons, and to receive in their minds for the most part the very opposite of those which we should wish them to have when they are grown up?

The burden is upon the broadcaster and the educator who would create the visual experience. And it is also upon those of us who would evaluate and become more selective in the use of the television "teacher."

REFERENCES

Clark, C.C. *Communication, Conflict, and the Portrayal of Ethnic Minorities: A Minority Perspective.* Unpublished manuscript, Stanford, University, 1972.

Comstock, George. "The Evidence So Far." *Journal of Communication,"* Vol. 25, 1974, pp. 25-34.

Gerbner, G. "Violence in Television Drama: Trends and Symbolic Functions." George Comstock and E.A. Rubinstein (Eds.). *Television and Social Behavior (Media Content and Control, Vol. 1),* Washington D.C.: U.S. Government Printing Office, 1972.

Kaye, Evelyn. *The Family Guide to Children's Television—What to Watch, What to Miss, What to Change and How to Do It.* New York: Pantheon Books, Random House, 1974.

Lesser, Gerald S. *Children and Television—Lessons from Sesame Street.* New York: Random House, 1974.

Liebert, R., Neale, John, and Davidson, Emily. *The Early Window.* New York: Permagon Press.

Liebert, R. and Poulos, R. *Television As a Moral Teacher—Man and Morality.* New York: Holt, Rinehart and Winston, 1973.

Toffler, Alvin. *Future Shock.* New York: Bantam Books, Inc., 1974, p. 281.

IX.

YOUNG CHILDREN AND THE ENVIRONMENT OF SCIENCE

By George T. Ladd

Any discussion about young children appropriately begins with the basic ingredient—the child. Youngsters like to be thought of as individuals. Accordingly, we shall initiate our consideration of young children by referring to an individual child.

Gregory and His World

Five-year-old Gregory is considered a very special person by his parents and grandparents. He is not only extremely cute, but he is also unusually bright and humorous. To those outside the family he would be called a normal child. The term "normal" often generates lively discussions among educators and parents alike. In this essay you will be allowed to form your own operational definition of normality by finding out more about Greg.

Greg possesses many qualities that are shared by others his age. Young children throughout the world may have different physical features, they might speak different languages or even play different games, but nonetheless, as humans they act and react to their environments in much the same manner.

Greg has just turned 5. He has blond hair, brown eyes and stands three feet, four inches tall. What is he like? Well, he is very much aware of *his* world. This world includes his parents, his brothers, his grandparents, his friends, and his acquaintances. His physical world, both indoors and out, also encompasses the sights, sounds, smells, touches and tastes of food, flowers, wind, rain, television, dirt and everything else imaginable.

One might wonder why Greg is so aware of his environment. The reason is that he, like all higher forms of animals, has the ability to gather stimuli from his surroundings through the use of his senses. His observations allow him to gather huge amounts of data about his encounters with the environment. The list of things he might experience in a given day runs the gamut from watching an ant carry a dead fly to discovering what happens when he throws dirt in the air.

Although Greg can understand his direct and concrete experiences, he has some difficulty with the more abstract ideas he encounters. He knows, for example, that Grandma makes delicious raspberry pies, but he does not know how long it will take to get to her house in New York or even where New York is! He knows that he will go swimming tomorrow but unless he is told that tomorrow is after his dark time nap, he does not comprehend. One soon discovers that although Greg's world seems vast, it does have very distinct boundaries. He knows the immediate world around him. What he has not experienced directly can only be conveyed to him by what he once said: "Tell me in words that I can understand and then I will know."

To Greg, knowing is synonymous with doing and he is always doing something. The source of this activity has created a controversy about the prime motivating energy of young children. Is there something innate that produced this seemingly constant activity, or is it the things in his environment that excite him and cause him to be an alert, active learner? There is a growing trend toward recognizing that young children, while they have a great deal in common with each other, possess a wide range of responses to a number of different energy sources. In Greg's case it seems that the motivation varies from time to time and from situation to situation.

Internally, Greg is motivated by several energies, the first of which is *curiosity*. His curiosity is a force which propels him into direct interactions with his environment. Although he doesn't realize it, Greg's level of curiosity is much higher than that of adults or even older children because he has not yet learned to eliminate what we would consider irrelevant or distracting material from his perceptions. This higher level of inquisitiveness makes Greg more conscious of his experiences and thus more responsive to his environment. If he were asked to list his observations about something as simple as a burning candle, his list would generally be two to three times *longer* than an adult's.

Greg's curiosity is not only at a high level, but it is also persistent. Endless *how's, why's, when's, where's, who's and what's* are generated by his contacts with the environment. His open, fresh and inquisitive attitude enable Greg to gain valuable perceptions about his experiences. These perceptions are the key to his intellectual growth, for they allow him to visualize relationships, categorize, discriminate, and generalize from his observations and direct experiences.

A second source of Greg's internal motivational energy is a drive toward *mastery*. His active explorations provide him with new experiences. These result in new information which, when added to that already acquired, expands his picture of the world. Greg's efforts to attain mastery of his world are exemplified by his persistent interaction with the environment. In carrying out his explorations, he places each new observation into the repository of his own past knowledge. No one else has or will experience the world in quite the same way he does. In the analysis, Greg will determine the real order in his environment. For Greg, mastery of his environment is part of a cycle; it reinforces activity that generates increased curiosity, persistence, and further master. As he gains increased competence, he is encouraged to investigate further.

The what of these investigations, while not classed as internal energy, is very important to our description of Greg for it describes the external stimuli that in turn stimulates his curiosity. The objects of his interactions cover a full range of items and events, but essentially they are those things which he experiences *directly* rather than *abstractly*. He formulates perceptions on the touchable, smellable, tasteable and other concrete realities of his world. If he has had no direct experience with something, it simply does not exist for him. He might be able to tell you that there is water in the air, but unless he can see it, he does not really grasp the concept.

The Learning Environment

Now that we have a clearer picture of Greg and his world, it is time to examine the learning environment for such children as it existed in the past and as it is being created today.

Approximately 15 years ago, both parents and educators were in agreement about what should happen in the years *before* a child entered formal schooling. They felt that the child did not have the intellectual capability to acquire cognitive skills, and believed that until the time of formal education, schooling should be avoided. This practice was based on the belief that the child should have time to mature both physically and mentally. In order to facilitate this process, the child's time should be devoted to play and enjoyment, not learning!

This approach was not as disastrous as some people claim. Young children, because of their sense of curiosity and other characteristics, still acquired a fantastic amount of knowledge about their environment. When they were ready for first grade, they still displayed that same curiosity, persistence, and need for mastering their environments.

But the classroom environment that greeted them was not very stimulating. It had a number of distinguishing features:

(1)   The drab colors and the rows of desks and other physical decor was unexciting. The teacher dominated the room and spent most of the time talking to the children and conveying knowledge to them.

(2)   The world presented to the child in school was the teacher's world. This frequently bore little resemblance to the child's own perceptions.

(3)   The children were primarily involved in activities which dealt with mastery, but they had few opportunities to carry out self-discovery on things which were of interest to them.

(4)   Most of the activities centered on the classroom, often negating a major portion of the young child's outdoor world.

(5)   Each student in the room received basically the same information at the same time, at the same rate, and in the same manner.

(6)   The knowledge which was transmitted to them was fragmented into such artificial divisions as reading, mathematics and social studies.

(7)   Parental involvement in the educative process was rare; mothers and fathers were generally consulted only if severe problems developed.

The effects of this learning environment on children like Gregory were predictable. John Dewey once said that no one has ever explained why children are so full of questions *outside* of school. The children indeed asked fewer questions, because so many of their questions were not answered. As the fun and the spontaineity were removed from learning, the *why's* began to disappear. The *what* they worked with became the most important priority. A number of children had difficulty with the continual flow of verbal symbols which they had to assimilate each day. As a result of this and other factors, a foreign, non-integrated, and sterile world was substituted for their own. Their curiosity was stifled along with their desire to master a larger environment.

Not *all* first grade classrooms were of the type previously described.

Many children learned a great deal in these environments, and some children whose learning styles were compatible with that style of education flourished. But the entire focus of the educational effort was on the adult's world, not the child's. In the final analysis this prohibited many children from realizing their full potential.

New Learning Settings for the New Children

During the past 10 years, a great amount of research and writing has been done about the young child and his educational needs. Changes in the educational environment have enabled parents and educators to gain a better perception of the child's world. This has led to further investigations of the causes of children's curiosity, persistence, and mastery. It has also led to inquiries about how these traits can be used to provide an educational environment that will facilitate the child's development. These new efforts seek to place the child at the center of the educatonal environment, rather than mold him into something that will fit *our* educational environment. In emphasizing the child, the problem now becomes one of definition, creation, and maintenance of an environment within which he or she can function as an individual and grow in the affective, cognitive and psychomotor domains.

Such an environment contains the following characteristics:

(1)   It recognizes the child's proven ability and eagerness to learn *before* he enters the first grade.

(2)   It provides a physical framework through which the child, interacting with others, can develop functional attitudes of rationality, honesty, objectivity, and humility.

(3)   It has a strong influence on the quality of the child's intellectual development.

(4)   It stimulates the child's natural curiosity leading him to observe, carry out self-discovery, master his world, and communcate his findings to others.

(5)   It *includes* the outside world, rather than closing it off.

(6)   It recognizes that the parent is a critical individual in the education process.

The above attributes are not inclusive, but represent many of the distinguishing features of the environment.

It then remains to determine *who* establishes such an environment and *where* it can be established. If one accepts the premise that children are capable of learning before they begin their formal education, then one must also accept parental involvement in the process both at home and in school. This view represents a marked departure from the past, but has been supported in theory and in practice during recent years.

By virtue of exposure time, intimacy, and potential knowledge of the child, parents hold the key to the period of development that precedes arrival at the nursery school or kindergarten door. Through patience, displays of interest, introduction to activities, and an acquisition of some understanding of the nature of young children, the parent fosters the child's continuing perfection of skills. Parents also provide an effective means by which the home and the school can be linked. A very real problem of the past has been the teacher's attempt to make accomodations for the child without any knowledge of the child or of the child's environment. With parental involvement, both inside and outside the classroom, this problem has been overcome. Parental involvement has also resulted in the additional benefits of the parent's experiences, interests and background.

The teacher, however, is still a most essential influence on the child's explorations into the more abstract world. The teacher must be able to assess the needs of the child and understand his motivations, as well as his immediate past environment. He or she must be able to sustain and, whenever possible, enhance the natural energies of the child through the creation and maintenance of a properly oriented school environment.

The Role of Science

How do parents and teachers create a viable learning environment? There are many ways in which to answer this question, but before doing so it is worthwhile to reflect again on the child and his world as described earlier. What does his immediate world contain? What does he do with his time? What things excite him? What does he ask questions about? These and other queries form the basis of a critical review that returns to the child. The parent and the teacher must attempt to meet the child and go outward from his world with him, instead of imposing their perspective of the world on him.

The child's world is inextricably associated with science. His experiences with thunder, ants, leaves, rocks, clouds, sun, sights, sounds and tastes can be categorized more precisely as objects of *investigation*. It is the process of investigation, of using one's senses to observe and formulate perceptions toward mastery of one's environment that is the essence of science. Science is an *activity* of man, spurred by his natural curiosity to find out more, to bring order to his life. As a result of this activity he is able to extend outward into unknown abstract worlds. The link between the child and science is more basic than its objects and processes, however, for curiosity is not only the prime motivating energy of the child, but also the inspiration of the natural sciences.

Since scientific investigation is a normal way for a child to learn about his world, we can look to it as a means through which to establish an educational environment; indoors and outdoors; both at home and at school. Science can assist the child in the acquisition of knowledge of the world while also increasing skill development. It provides alternatives which allow the parent and the teacher to create the environment which meets the criteria listed on page 155.

A parent can contribute to the child's introduction to science in a number of ways by:

(1) allowing the child to experience an activity by himself and then talking with him about it,

(2) being involved with the child from the beginning of the activity and then discussing his observations with him,

(3) allowing the child to work with a small group of children and following up on their work.

Whatever method is used, it is important that active investigation be included, as well as the communication of questions and observations. The relationship of parent to child in this effort should be one of partnership. Patience in the questioning process is critically important. The child should be given time to think about an answer or even time to come up with another question. Another practice involves the formulation of general questions such as "What did *you* see?" "What do *you* think happened?" "Why do *you* think....?" These questions place the child at the center of the experience and allow him to bring his own observations and knowledge to bear. This contrasts with the common mistake of raising a series of leading questions which forces the child to give the *right* answer (which is always yours, not the child's). Still another practice which should be employed, particularly when the parent is faced with such questions as "What is electricity?" is the avoidance of furnishing answers in abstract terms. Instead of telling him the answer, which he will not be able to comprehend, refer him to the things which electricity does. This refocuses him on the concrete and avoids the abstract concept of electrical energy until a time when he can comprehend it.

Home Activities

The following list will give parents some ideas for possible sources of activities for the child:

Indoors

In either an apartment or a house, a very rich environment of science objects and experiences can be created for the young child.

(1) *Aquaria:*   made with anything from empty jars to expensive, fully equipped containers capable of holding water, plants, snails, fish, and sand. These provide the child with a world not often open to him.

(2) *Terraria:*   desert, woodland, bog, or any mixture of these with plants or small animal life—can create a micro environment where natural outdoor conditions can be duplicated.

(3) *Animals:*   many small animals, including insects, reptiles, amphibians, birds, and mammals (hamsters, guinea pigs and gerbils) can be kept within the confines of one's home, creating a direct and responsible relationship between the child and the animal.

(4) *Plants:*   given proper growing conditions, a myriad of plants can be grown and maintained providing another opportunity for the child to witness the life process.

(5) *Records:*   the sounds of nature and other scientific phenomena can be conveyed through this medium. Records add to the child's involvement with science activity and incorporate sound as a vehicle in his learning.

(6) *Cooking:*   often overlooked as a science experience; food and its preparation involve measuring, classifying and observation. There are many foods that the young child can prepare with or without the aid of a parent. A unique satisfaction can result from eating the results of the experiments.

(7) *Pictures:*   the use of photos and sketches can lead to observations, questions and discussions about untold areas of the child's more immediate and abstract environments.

(8) *Books:*   books with colored illustrations can bring the child an increased awareness of the world.

(9) *Filmstrips:*   similar to books, filmstrips broaden awareness. These can often be rented, along with projectors from the local library.

(10) *Drawing:*   a very individualist and active way for the child to make his environment come alive—drawing is a basic means of communicating with others about one's world.

(11) *Toys:*   currently much research points to the significance of toys as vehicles for self-development. A variety of science-related toys can be used.

(12) *Storytelling:*   this can be used to integrate both the real and the fantasy worlds of science. The parent can help the child discern the difference between the two. After an appropriate introduction, the child can often begin to create his own stories.

(13) *Television:*   the television networks have in recent years increased the number of special and regular shows which open up the vast worlds of science to the young child.

In addition to the items already discussed, there remains the domain of interior decorating. For example, bulletin boards can be used for collections of feathers, rocks, leaves, and other specimens. Such collections can be used to reinforce the interaction between the child and his environment.

Outdoors

There are numerous possibilities for the indoor world, but the outdoor environment offers a rich, almost limitless, source of exciting stimuli. Explorations into woods, vacant lots, parks, beaches, ponds and other areas provide a wealth of opportunities for discovering and learning. The child should discover some things for himself, but should also be shown things which he might not fully understand or notice on his own. For example, one can ask him what might have caused the cracks in the sidewalk. Or, he could be asked to name some of the things a bird uses to build a nest. Let him use all of his senses, ask him questions and let him see. Remember that seemingly insignificant things can mean a great deal for the child; do not stand in the way. Everything has tremendous potential for learning.

For purposes of this chapter, outdoors includes science museums, aquaria, planetaria, zoos, airports, construction sites, and factories. As an aid in exploring these locations, a simple camera can be used for the child to take pictures of the things that interest him. Similarly, pencils, paper to draw upon, and a bag in which to collect things sustain the learning process long after the initial experience is over. Picture taking, drawing, and collecting provide a link between the environment of the outdoors and that of the indoors. The parent, through his communication with the child, integrates the two worlds.

Classroom Activities

The school, whether it is a nursery school, a day care center, a kindergarten or even a first grade, should actually be an extension of the home environment. The classroom, in the final analysis, simply expands the number and kinds of learning opportunities.

In addressing the needs of the students, two criteria should be emphasized. First, simply devoting time to the study of science does not necessarily use science to its full potential as an agent for the intellectual development of the child. The world of the child is not fragmented into art, reading, math; it is integrated. As such, science should be used to aid in the acquisition of all types of skills. Second, the teacher, like the parent, is the creator of an environment. There is more involved in encouraging the development of the child than the acquisition of animals or the arrangement of field trips. The teacher, like the parent, must be aware that the general relationship with the child is critical. The teacher's attitude, pacing of activities, and degree of involvement set him apart as a professional. Since he deals with a new group of students each year, he must gain information about the students as quickly as possible in order to create the best possible atmosphere for them.

Closer relationship between the teacher and the parent contribute significantly to the learning environment. The two must work in a cooperative and a complimentary manner. The home and the school should no longer be separate experiences but should be extensions of one another.

Science in the classroom, like the science activities associated with the home, provide opportunities that invite the child's active involvement. Since science is a way of perceiving the world, the student must interact with the materials presented to him in order to perceive and draw conclusions about the world. A selection of science materials for young children should follow these guidelines:

(1)   Safe under all conditions for use.

(2)   Should range from simple materials—sand, water, balloons—to more complex materials such as buzzers and pulleys.

(3)   Should provide examples of concepts or clusters of phenomena such as color, taste, or other sense impressions.

(4)   Should include a size and a degree of complexity that the child can handle.

(5)   Should bear a direct relationship with the child's environment.

(6) Should place the emphasis on the use of materials.

(7) Should adapt to the child's changing interests.

Science can be brought into the classroom in a number of ways. The following methods do not include the aquaria, terraria and other science experiences previously discussed under home activities. These activities can and should be done in the classroom, but the following list is limited to those that can be done with greater ease in a classroom setting.

Science and Play

A child spends a great deal of time involved in what can be termed as "play." When one looks at what a child plays with, he discovers that they are not always commercially produced toys. Instead, they are often "things" from the child's world. A teacher can introduce science into the child's play by providing such things as:

(1) A pulley system in the block area.

(2) Opportunities to grow things as well as to play with animals in the classroom.

(3) A magnifying glass and magnets.

(4) Bells, buzzers and flashlights.

Science Demonstrations

Demonstrations of things with which the child cannot become directly involved himself are an effective means of fostering inquiry. An example of a typical demonstration might involve showing the children what happens when an ice cube is placed in a glass of rubbing alcohol in contrast to its behavior in a glass of water. (It sinks in the alcohol because ice is heavier than the alcohol.) The demonstration should be carried out in a simplified fashion and should be directed at the concrete not the abstract. It should be followed by student discussions developed through student and teacher questions. The teacher initiated questions should not be of the "20 question" variety, because the experience will degenerate into a story-telling affair. Instead, they should stimulate the student's creative thinking processes: What did you see? Why do you think that happened? The teacher should know all the science behind the demonstration, but he or she should not necessarily impart all of this to the child.

Recording of Science Experiences

The child should be encouraged to record his observations. This can be done through drawings or even tape recorders. These records are an important part of "sciencing."

Science Corners

Some teachers prefer to devote one area of the room for science materials. The author discourages the practice of isolating science from other portions of the classroom environment. Since the child's world is integrated, then it follows that the school environment should reflect this. While there may be a water play area or a sand box area where it is easier, safer, or more convenient to carry out some activities, displays and science involvement should not be isolated, but spread around the classroom.

Displays of Science

(1) *Science bulletin boards* should be designed for *use,* not just for display. There should, of course, be things to look at, but there should also be materials to taste, touch, smell, and hear. A sequential display can be arranged to show things as they grow, melt or cook. Items which can be compared and contrasted should be included as well.

(2) *Science tables* can be used effectively to stimulate interest and self-discovery. Rocks, leaves, lenses, magnets and other materials allow the child to acquire direct science experience. Such displays stimulate a child's curiosity which is so necessary for his continued development.

Science and the Senses

Through the use of his senses, the young child moves in, around and outside his world. His dependence on sensory activities enables him to gain greater sophistication in observational and other process skills.

(1) *Smell:* Many substances can be used to explore safely the odors in the environment, including items with no apparent smell. Items can be supplied by the teacher, the students or both. Students can draw comparisons between the objects they smell, relate to their classmates the results of their experiences, and devise their own system of classifying the odors. This task should be progressively complex for the student. One should begin with familiar smells with the object in view, follow to

familiar odors with the object out of view, and finally introduce objects with unfamiliar odors. Students should enjoy the number of games which this activity can provide. They can even eat those objects which are edible and combine several sense experiences.

(2) *Taste:* With the proper safeguards, this sense can form the basis of a large number of activities. Different foods can be used quite effectively to develop observational skills. As with the sense of smell, the activities should be devised to isolate the sense of taste from the other senses, so that the child's attention is focused on that single sense. Again, this process should get progressively complex; the child should be introduced to unfamiliar foods in order to expand his world of taste.

(3) *Touch:* The soft, smooth, prickly, slimy world of touch has a number of possibilities for perfecting the child's observational skills. Teachers can use a variety of materials with a full range of textures. The child can then compare the textures and devise his own system of description and classification.

(4) *Sound:* Beginning with the familiar and moving to the unfamiliar the child should be exposed not only to differing sound intensities and pitch, but also to the relationship of the sound to the producer. Resources can include animals, plants, dried leaves, a branch breaking, wind, rain, bells, rocks, and water. First preference should be given to natural sounds followed by movement toward increasingly difficult sound association activities.

(5) *Sight:* The size, shape, color or any other discernable attributes of an object can provide innumerable experiences with the sense of sight. As with all sensory experiments, the child should not only become involved with the objects in question, but should also be asked to verbalize his reactions and observations to this classmates. Teachers should encourage a child to bring in his own materials and to invent his own words and classifications.

Each of the five sense modalities can provide the young child with a full range of manipulative experiences and related communicative skills dealing with the identification, classification and differentiation of activities. In communicating these experiences the child could employ simple narration techniques as well as the dramatic technique of imitation. The activities can take place in a structured or non-structured setting and the teacher should ensure that one type of structure does not receive attention at the expense of the other.

Conclusion

There are, of course, as many methods of dealing with science and indeed all subjects of interest, as there are teachers. Many people have devoted their lives to the education of young children. There is one who stands out in my memory. This woman was in the final year of a 25 year career as a nursery school teacher when I spoke with her. In our conversation I made reference to the "new" young children and she surprised me by saying that she had a real problem with that terminology. She proposed that children are the same as they have always been, no matter where they live. It is the child who has always been the *given;* the variables have been the adults' perceptions of them and the educational-social environment they have created for children.

In reflecting on her comment, I must agree. The new child is based on our understanding of the "new" environment, the environment which provides a means by which the child can realize his full potential. The previous essays on intelligence, testing, learning problems and disabilities, play, morals and values, and sexual development and identity have communicated that the child is *not* a mass of unmolded clay to be shaped only by external forces. Instead, he or she is a unique individual who brings to the world unique characteristics. It is our responsibility to better understand the child and not the child's duty to adapt to our world. Our task is to create an environment within which he can experience the 'things' that will make up his world. Science can be a very important part of the environment for two reasons. It can be used to create and maintain an environment conducive to growth. And because science is a part of the child, it is a way of looking at things that enables the child to expand his knowledge and bring order to this world.

REFERENCES

Banet, Barbara, *et al. The Scrap Book,* Ann Arbor, Michigan: Friends of Perry Nursery School, 1972. This work is a collection of activities for preschoolers. It is written by both teachers and parents and contains a variety of activities suited for 3-, 4- and 5-year-olds in many kinds of home and school settings. The materials required for most of the activities are household scraps and the reader can find an extensive material index to assist in recycling these items.

Cobb, Vicki. *Science Experiments You Can Eat,* Philadelphia: J.B. Lippincott Co., 1972. Book contains 30 activities which provide a way for children to explore the world of foods and how they can be used to carry out scientific inquiry. Children can find out what makes popcorn pop, how rock candy is made and how to make grape jelly among others. The reader is not only instructed as to how to perform the "experiment," but also told *why* it works. Valuable for home and school.

Croft, Doreen J. and Hess, Robert D. *An Activities Handbook For Teachers of Young Children,* Boston: Houghton Mifflin Co., 1975, p. 198. This revised enlarged spiral-bound handbook provides the teachers with a number of proven activities which will foster teaching skills in the areas of art, math, science, language arts and cooking. Other experiments ai' designed to encourage creativity and to maintain the child's interest level. Althoug.ı most of the activities are tailored for classrooms, they can be used by parents at home or other locations outside of the "school."

Hess, Robert D. and Croft, Doreen J. *Teachers of Young Children,* Boston: Houghton Mifflin Co., 1975, 2nd edition. This book is for and about teachers who work with young children. It gives the teacher or potential teacher in the field of early childhood education a theoretical, attitudinal and practical instructional basis. It is a methods type test without an emphasis on activities, but rather the approaches and problems which one might employ.

Marzollo, Jean, and Lloyd, Janice. *Learning Through Play,* New York: Harper Colophon Books, 1972. Publication is directed at parents who wish to help preschoolers learn at ho;ne. It is written in terms the layman will understand and provides the reader with insights into early childhood education. A wide variety of well illustrated activities for parents to involve their children with are included.

Riles, Wilson C. *ECE In California Passes Its First Tests,* Phi Delta Kappa, September 1975, Vol. 57, pp.3-7. This article chronicles the efforts in California, which began in the fall of 1973, to implement a vary massive state wide education reform in early childhood education, kindergarten through third grade. It is written by the superintendent of public instruction who conceived and carried out this move toward a comprehensive early education program that incorporates parents as an integral part of the classroom environment. The review provides the reader with a summary of the initial assessment program showing excellent results from these reforms.

This book was composed with Greylock's in-house Compugraphic Unified Composer® editing terminal and Unisetter® phototypesetter. The text typeface is English Times and the titles and headings appear in Paladium.